C000021282

Educational Reforms and their Attainment Outcomes

Tore Lindbekk

EDUCATIONAL REFORMS AND THEIR ATTAINMENT OUTCOMES

The Norwegian Reform Experience 1955–1975

Tapir
Academic Press

© Tapir Academic Press, Trondheim 2001

ISBN 82-519-1697-6

This publication may not be reproduced, stored in a retrieval system or transmitted in any form or by any means; electronic, electrostatic, magnetic tape, mechanical, photo-copying, recording or otherwise, without permission.

Digital production by Tapir trykkeri

TAPIR ACADEMIC PRESS

N–7005 TRONDHEIM, Norway

Tel: 73 59 32 10
Fax: 73 59 32 04
E-mail: forlag@tapir.no
http://www.tapir.no/forlag

Content

Preface

The postwar reforms of the Norwegian educational system were radical as well as extensive. New conceptions of what schooling should comprise were brought to bear upon the content and organization of the Norwegian school from the primary stage up to universities. These conceptions were parts of a broad all-European movement. But the norwegian policies went farther than the parallels in other countries.

Although the reforms were scarcely coordinated, some ideas were central to all of them: schooling should be for all youths, even those with limited financial resources or personal capacity. All should have a fair chance, even in relation to the highest reaches of the school system. And an unification of the various parts of the system should take place, to make for better use of the resources and the creation of the widest possible span of opportunities for the individual student.

In this work we take stock of this reform complex. We desire to measure whether the reformers succeeded in their attempts. Our first question is: how many accomplished an education on the various stages of the system? Using this approach we are able to assess as a success the part of the reform that consisted in the establishing of secondary schools in all those municipalities which had no such facilities prior to the reform. In a similar vein, we observe increases in educational attainments in the counties who had no universities, but now were invited (by other means) to become fully-fledged members of the higher education society. The shorter school year introduced in 1973 and 1974 does, however, present some difficulty when assessing the upper secondary education reform.

Even more important was the fact that the reforms were intended to produce greater equality between social strata, geographical locations and genders. Here our conclusions are safer. Our data allow us to claim that the (upper and lower) secondary reforms especially mobilized women and youths from dispersed (rural) population areas for school attainments. So that the backwardness of these strata were eliminated. The reforms supported and added to the general trends for these strata. But it is doubtful if the reforms served to produce more equality between social classes or between families with different amounts of «educational capital».

August 2001
Tore Lindbekk

1

THE INTERNATIONAL CONTEXT OF THE REFORMS

Ambitions.

The idea of an equal and common education for all citizens, is closely associated with the idea of a democratic society, and is mostly taken for granted in countries and regions with a long folkeskole tradition, like Germany and Scandinavia (Green 1990, Rust 1989). - Here a common school, subjected to the authority of the state, was part of the modern nation-building «project».

In the course of the 19th and early 20th centuries, seven years of compulsory, common-for-all education was established in all the Nordic countries. Common schooling up to age 12 or more was even realized in Germany, France and Great Britain (but in these countries sizeable numbers attended private or ecclesiastical schools).

After the Second World War, the endeavours to create a school system that was «equal» and «common» entered into a new phase. The age for leaving school was raised. However, the new school concept went beyond that. It also related to the broader reaches of the educational system. The conception of an equal schooling for all also was brought to bear upon administrative structures, school buildings, curricular content, and instructional procedures. Dahlløf summed up the main items of the new, radicalized policy this way (Dahlløf 1990:177):

> *1.Horisontal administrative integration: all education at the same stage should be*

subordinated to one common political/adminstrative agency.

2.Vertical administrative integration: the agencies in charge of the most "common" (=lower) part of the system, should extend their authority to higher stages.

3.Physical integration: the various lines and specialties (on the same level) should have their schooling in the same building and be served by one common staff.

4.Curricular integration: there should be more common stuff for all students on the same stage, to some extent also across stages.

5.Standardization of resource inputs: instruction time, equipment and other facilities should be of equal amount for all students on the same stage of education.

6.Fewer lines: General educations are preferable to specialized educations that prepare for specialized purposes, whether particular occupations or particular further educations.

7.Pedagogical integration: streaming/grouping/tracking according to ability should stop, also repetition of stages for those who for some or other reason were not up to the demands presented.

8.Gratis schooling: school fees should be abolished. The public authorities also should provide financial support for students.

The reason for the parallel developments between various countries, that was pointed out by Dahlløf, may have been that a particular "logic" by now was built firmly into the education systems: resting upon particular conceptions among the politicians, implicit in the authorities' planning procedures as well as the arguments of particular interest groups; it was a question of premises that noone any more resisted; maybe also a side-effect of the welfare-state that by now was under construction.

The new educational policies included expansions of the existing systems as well as qualitative upgradings. - But the visions of the reformers related to a much broader set of social concerns than that of more (and steadily more equal) schooling for all; Leschinsky and Mayer (1990:17-18) have summed up the thinking behind the comprehensive movement in West Germany by these points:

1. Keeping the educational paths open until the end of the primary school (age fourteen).

2. An integrated school with a broad range of subjects and other services, to help the individual progress.

3. Better development of the talent reserves.

4. Production of social cohesion via the experience of being a commonity of learners.

5. Neutralize the existing social handicaps. Equal opportunity for all.

In their presentations of the English debates on the subject, Ford 1969 and Bellaby 1977:19-23, mainly stressed points 1, 3, 5, and a variant of 2 relating to continuity with working class culture. Weeks 1986:5-13), emphasized points 1, 4, 5, and 2 relating to the furthering of equal prestige +to all types of talent. The Swedish reformers emphasized equality opportunity, equal prestige of knowledge areas, preparing for enlightened citizenship and the steady modernization of work life (Nilsson 1981:178-190, Marklund 1984, Erikson and Jonsson 1993).

*****

According to the Nordic conception of "enhetsskole", all varieties of education and training at a particular stage of schooling should be subordinated to the same administrative agency; and the individual school should be "broad" in content and in the student categories catered for.

This perspective at first was restricted to the reforms on the elementary level. But in the course of the postwar period it was extended to secondary and higher stages as well.

Sweden was in the forefront on most of the Dahlløf criteria: obligatory schooling up to age sixteen was established i 1962, in charge of the municipal educational authorities. The resources and time schedules of the schools were standardized, grouping and vocational programs were mostly eliminated on the elementary stage (up to age sixteen) as well as in the lower secondary school (ages fourteen to sixteen). On the upper secondary stage (ages seventeen to nineteen) common multi-programme schools were the rule from 1971, with mostly the same content all over the country.

These reforms were implemented during a period with great expansion in the educational system; on all stages the intakes of new students were increasing. The policies, therefore, could be expected to produce educational upgrading of the population as well as an evening out of differences between social classes and geographical areas. However, from the mid70s, the higher education expansion stopped in Sweden (Marklund 1984, Erikson & Jonsson 1993:51-73, Dahlløf, 1990). A more severe financial regime was brought to bear upon the educational system, and higher education numbers were subjected to labour market considerations. However, the principle of unification remained, with the municipality in charge of both primary and secondary education and one common administrative agency in charge of all the higher education institutions of the individual geographical region (län).

In France, compulsory schooling until age sixteen was established even earlier (1959). However, organizational unification of all schooling for ages eleven to sixteen was not attained until the 1970s; there were similar curricula but separate schools (colleges) for those planning to leave school after thqat stage, and one for those on the way to the upper secondary stage. (Prost 1990: 49-52). The new, common, college was even in the 1980s a theoretical school with a demanding curriculum. Retake of courses was an important part of the system, and during the last years of obligatory school, separate courses provided for students with further stages of schooling in mind and those who wanted to leave school after that stage (Duru-Bellah/Mingat 1990:65-88). The upper stage of secondary education was sustained as a purely academic programme for an elite group.

In Scotland, obligatory schooling up to age sixteen was established in the early 1960s, in some districts in the form of common schools. But the curricula were not uniform and streaming was common. But a homogenization of curricula was going on, and streaming was on the way out. Around 1980 the comprehensive principle covered all districts, with common curricula, and virtually no streaming or "creaming" (i.e. outlets to more selective schools or programmes (Gray 1990: 131-134).

The English and German reorganizations were much less extensive than those in Sweden and Scotland. In West Germany common schooling stopped at age twelve. After that the youth was allocated between the Realschule/Gymnasium, a "Hauptschule" similat to the Scandinavian continuation school ("framhaldsskole","fortsettelses-skole","folkehøg-skole") of the early postwar period, and vocational schooling, usually as a supplement to apprenticeship. Some municipalities in addition to this had comprehensive schools for families who for some reason wanted their children to stay on longer in a school less distinctively placed in the system, The city of Bremen went farther than this; established here was a comprehensive school for all youth aged twelve to sixteen (Leschinsky and Mayer 1990:13-25).

The English solutions differed between municipalities: some places the old separation between (more elitist) "public schools" and "secondary modern" schools was retained at the secondary stage, other places "comprehensive" principles were laid down. However, the curricula converged. The former practices with ability-separated "streams" or "tracks" was to a large extent abolished between the 1960s and the 1980s, but milder forms of organizational differentiation were retained within most schools (Gray 1990:115-119). Also, despite that the allowances from the authorities differed little between schools, the differences in the resources that were at hand, might be large; because some schools profited from large contributions from the parents, other had no such extra sources.

The English pattern also was complicated by the strong position of private education, which served about ten per cent of the cohort. During the 1980s, these schools were modernized and improved in several ways, and the number who opted for private education increased (Salter and Tapper 1985).

During the 1960s to 1980s, all these countries approached a common and comprehensive schooling up to age sixteen. During these developments, Sweden and Scotland generally were in the lead, England and West Germany behind, while France kept a middle position.

At the upper secondary stage, the changes were smaller. Most countries expanded their upper secondary student numbers (OECD 1985:12-13), but the gymnasia generally retained their traditional - mainly theoretical - content. In West Germany a well-working apprenticeship system was developed further, an important alternative to the gymnasium. During the 1970s and 1980s it received graduates from the gymnasium as well as from the Hauptschule.

But the most conspicuous new development on this stage came in Sweden; here an adminstrative integration of all schools on the upper secondary stage was realized. The new "gymnasieskola" had a three year academic line alongside with two shorter lines, with varying mixes of academic and vocationally oriented curricula. One wanted to keep the not so academically minded in school up to age eighteen, with connections to working life as well as to academic education.

The Norwegian reforms, to be treated more fully in the next chapter, went mostly parallel to the Swedish (sometimes they were a little behind). The reforms in Norway differed by their emphasis on geographical decentralization, their especially well-funded lower secondary stage ("youth school") and a much larger plurality of "lines" on the upper secondary stage. Important for the development of the system was also a steady expansion of student intakes even in the 1970s and 1980s (while a leveling off of numbers occurred came in Sweden).

Reform outcomes.

Were the reform outcomes on level with the reformers' expectations?

During most of the period, the reorganizations were paralleled by expansions. The intakes and student numbers went up at all stages. Also, some qualitive improvements of the educational services were realized: buildings were modernized; teaching equipment bettered; the training of teachers extended. Is not easy to separate the effect of these improvements from those of the school reforms.

Also we should consider some changes in the broader society; there were income increases, new welfare systems; during the first postwar decades also the living conditions of large parts of the population improved. Some demographic changes contributed to these developments; smaller families not only meant better material conditions for the remaining (and fewer) children, but also more attention to the individual child from his/her parents.

The most observable effect of all these changes was that the average levels of education went up (OECD 1985). It is more uncertain if redistributions of attainments occurred. The conclusion from some studies around 1980, was that the previous patterns of attainment distributions mostly were retained (Gray 1990). Swedish and Scottish studies around 1990 carried out some more detailed assessments of the reform effects; These studies indicated that some (small) changes in the direction of larger class equality of attainments had come about. Gamoran (1993) attributed the Scottish changes to an evening out of resource inputs and attainment goals between schools; according to Jonsson (1993), the Swedish changes reflected a long-term trend towards smaller class differences.

One large 13-nation study (Persistent Inequalities 1993) presented comparative data from a number of modern countries. It concluded that some reductions of attainment differences (i.e. by class and educational background) indeed had taken place in the course of the twentieth century; but these trends had petered out in the most recent period. The implication was: the general social, economic and demographic changes had produced some redistributions, but these changes came not during the period when the reform effects were expected to appear.

The processes that the reforms played into.

Whithin what context of processes and mechanisms functioned these reforms? Recent sociological research has widened our insight in the processes and causes that influence school policies and individual educational careers. Some elaborations of the reformers' assumptions appear here, as well as contradictions of some beliefs commonly held by experts and politicians.

The policies may be related to a large number of theories about the school - environment - student-dynamics. These theories can conveniently be arranged along two dimensions: one relating to school characteristics and how they model student behaviour and student conditions; the other considers community background and how the school and the individual student reflect such backgrounds.

The most general of the school-theories (or rather: implicit assumptions) relate to the socialization effects by schooling: learning as well as school motivation depends upon the amount of exposition to the experience of being in school. The more years the student spends within the school organization (or under its influence) the more he/she will be convinced that schooling is good for him/her. And the more eager he/she will be to learn more and desire advancement to ever higher stages of schooling. In the same vein, this impact depends on the resources commanded by the school.

During the 1950s and 1980s, such views were basic to the arguments for extension of compulsory schooling, and they were even advocated by some of those who were critical to the reforms: one will never be able to provide the amounts of resources needed to provide an «equalizing» service for all students, even those who are retarded or delinquent.

The rather small redistributional effects that followed the extension of compulsory schooling (and by that: the production of a more equal schooling across backgrounds) indicate that this view was unrealistic or incomplete. The experiences from Sweden and Scotland were especially impressive because the school systems of these countries came close to complete comprehensiveness: all versions of streaming were abolished. All students, therefore, might be said to have attained equal chances of getting «convinced».

How much counted the resource-factor for this effect of schooling for school-motivation? Can it be attained by just some brief encounters between student and teacher, for instance a couple of times per week? - How much count the number of student per class, the qualities of the teachers and the number of teacher-hours per student? During the 1970s the resources per upper secondary education student in the OECD countries was more than ten times the average for the 37 poorest countries (Coombs 1985:160). Within the poorest group a (positive) marginal effect seemed to have appeared even by small increases of resource inputs. In modern countries the picture was much less clear. The main conclusion from Mortimore and his colleagues' extensive follow up of pupils at 50 London schools was that junior schools with less than 24 pupils per class were more "effective" from the point of view of grades (three central school disciplines) than schools with larger classes (Mortimore et al. 1989:226); but the efficiency factor did not differentiate in relation to class, race or gender (1989: 206 -216). In a study of a more limited number of schools in London, Rutter 1979 found that the staff's "ethos" promoted learning; but in the same vein: the staff factor "boosted" the performances of all categories of students (Mortimore et al. p.209).

Both staff ethos and class sizes were probably correlated with a number of other "input" factors, financial as well as others. Hanushek et al. (1994) summarized the results of more than one hundred empirical studies (mainly in the US and Great Britain) of impacts of financial factors. His conclusion was that the trends commonly were unclear; but if differences in learning effect appeared, they might be explained by other factors, that were correlated with the considered input factors (mostly class size and teacher qualifications).

Gamoran partly attributed the equalization of attainments by the Scottish reforms (compulsory schooling for all until age 16, comprehensive organization of the schools - and no tracking) - not to the reorganizations and extension of a compulsory, common schooling, but larger equality of inputs, that is: more equal amounts of financial resources between schools - and more equal (uniform) contents of curricula.

Hanushek confirmed the existence of quality differences between schools, but stated that they are little related to expenditures, class sizes, students per teacher ratios or teacher qualifications (- commonly indexed by their salaries) (Hanushek et al.1994:30). - The studies that reported different out-comes by different resource inputs, used aggregated data (this even applied to Mortimore's and Gamoran's studies. TL's remark), and such analyses tend to "systematically overestimate the impacts of school expenditure-related properties on student attainment (Hanushek et al. 1994:29). - Maybe the homogenization of curricula, - another part of the Scottish reform, was as crucial for the attainment outcome as the equalization of resources (=school years and teacher-student ratios)?

The resources approach might be modified so as to emphasize the *differentiation* of inputs and of pedagogical tasks: students who differ much from the others in abilities and attitudes, need equipments and teaching methods that differ even more; this argument especially applies to students with particular handicaps; previously it generated special schools (for particular categories of handicap), special classes, or special programmes. Notable example: the Headstart Programme in the US (Ziegler and Muenchow 1992). See also the overview of special education policies in various countries (Special Education Reviewed 1996). However, it is difficult to find a simple way to index such differentiation, and the conclusions from the Headstart Programme were contested (Halsey 1980).
Ever since Coleman's study of attainment patterns in the US around 1960 (Coleman 1966), the "school class composition-theory" has been recurrent. Coleman's cross-national material showed that the school attainment of the individual student to a large extent varied by the number of coloured

students in the class. Knudsen's study of lower secondary schools grades in Bergen around 1970 (Knudsen 1977) showed a similar effect in Norway (in this study the proportion from working class background was a main variable), even after a large number of other individual conditions had been accounted for.

The implication of these findings seemed to be that educational "improvements" for students from poor or little privileged background was conditional upon a breaking up of school districts and school intake routines. By composing school classes so that they mirror the total population, one will attain a "lifting up" of the attainments of the less advantaged as well as a depression of those from particularly advantaged backgrounds.

Comprehensive thinking got a support by Coleman's findings. In their generalized form these findings implied that ability-based streaming or tracking generally should stop (and by that, the students' learning conditions would become more equal); Even handicapped students should attend "normal" classes. - The bussing programme in the US was a particularly radical version of policies following these conclusions. - But the programme did not produce changes commensurate with the magnitude of the reform itself. More recent studies of the impacts of mixed ability-classes compared with more homogenous classes failed to turn out significant evidence that particular talent categories profited more than others by one rather than another organization pattern (Gjesme 1994).

- But another observation ·was that the teachers found teaching in heterogenous classes more demanding. This view may have influenced the recruitments and motivations of teachers; selective recruitment of teachers may be the "real" reason for the recurrent observation that "grouping" was associated with more «unequal» attainments. Hallinan (1994) argued similarly: the class composition-effect observed in previous research, was produced by input differences; the classes who mainly had good students, got better service than those with weak or troublesome students.

However, it might be argued: even this argument, that "composition" is not the crucial variable, but the way resources are allocated within the school, should be expected to diminish over time, as a side-effect of the reform itself. Because the authorities (in obedience to current thinking) subjected more resources to an equality of outcome principle (and put steadily more resources into services for «unprivileged») the discomforts for the teachers in question should be expected to diminish.

A quite different perspective on school characteristics was presented in Kerckhof's (1993) observations that school buildings function as "inert fields": buildings from earlier school periods were crystallization points for - one might even say icons of - exclusion or inclusion, embedded in the collective memories of neighbourhoods. Spaces and places had deeper meanings than represented in rational considerations. Buildings that housed grammar schools in earlier period, retained their repellant force for working class youth, despite recent introductions of activities and role models designed to welcome all varieties of youth.

Kerckhof's argument is plausible. But in so far as it is correct, the processes described should only apply to schools with a history, schools with roots in the pre-comprehensive period, not to quite new schools and school buildings. Therefore, these processes will fade away as new school buildings become more numerous. Implication of this: the immediate effects of the reforms might be small, but more visible impacts will appear in the longer run.

*****

The view that particular school properties determined attainment distributions was commonly associated with ideas that particular (individual) backgrounds factors influenced the students' school interests and attitudes to the learning process, the teachers and the school generally.

An early observation was that the attainment outcomes varied by social/-cultural backgrounds. Explanation: the goals and values of various strata differ (Hyman 1957, Parsons 1959, Willis 1981); and because of that will schooling, school knowledge and the career effects of schooling be appreciated differently. - Another variant of the theory: particular cultural facilities are distributed unequally among the various strata, for instance books and mastery of the languages or language codes of the school (Atkinson 1985); students from some backgrounds are advantaged, those from other backgrounds disadvantaged, and the educational outcomes will vary in the same way. In a third version more fundamental (usually: unconscious) differences in attitudes and educational predispositions are emphasized (Bourdieu 1987, Darnell and Hoem 1996:275-283); these attitudes are long-term reflexes of collective experiences of power inequality - and will produce attainment differences even after the initial differences in resources and power have vanished.

These value and culture-theories are not easily separable from each other. But they may be differentiated by the time perspectives implied: some theories relate to quite particular differences in value premises, that reflect present conditions and may change after current conditions (- for instance labour market conditions) change; other theories relate to more basic and stable predispositions, that only may change in the course of generations.

More pertinent terms for these two factors might be: "patterns of preference" – that may change even in the short run, and "pattern of culture" basic personality traits, that are more deeply rooted and for that reason less mallable.

These theories have mainly been presented to account for class differences in educational attainment; but may also apply to differences on the basis of gender, ethnicity and home locality. Some authors (Bourdieu 1973, Haavelsrud 1984, Fürst 1988) made these theories parts of extensive theories about class conflicts, center-periphery conflict or gender conflict.

- Boudon (1973) pointed out that differences between various strata in school behaviour might be described from the point of view of more particularistic orientations: schooling endangers or furthers (positively valued) social connections to particular people: among university-educated strata is higher education is a condition for preserving this belongingness; other strata consider such education a threat to such belongingness. Otherwise stated: the preferences by various strata may be considered to be identical; they relate to the gaining of respect from particular persons and communities, and to sustain their belongingness to particular networks. But the persons, communities and networks they relater to, are differentially located; the actions and procedures chosen will therefore differ as well. The experiences from studies of the educational attainments of immigrant children may seem to throw some doubt on theories that particular strata or minorities are «foreigners» within the educational system, and therefore doomed to failure. With the exception for prestations in the "mother language"(i.e. that of the receiving country), immigrant children commonly have attained grades close to the levels of "natives" - at least after the researchers have corrected for social class and/or parents' educational status (Fuligni 1997, Similä 1994, Vallet and Caille 1996, Lauglo 1997). Even the hypothesis of attainment differences between immigrant groups of Confucian descent and immigrants from oriental cultures lacking the Confucian book reverence, failed to survive closer investigation. A recent Oslo investigation observed a small attainment handicap among immigrant pupils from "the third world, but also that the social class factor had smaller impact than within the majority population (Krange and Bakken 1998). - The "doubly disadvantaged" working class youth from the third world attained on level with (or even better than) Norwegian working class children. It is interesting that this conclusion is close to the observations during a classical study of school adjustments among the culturally extremely "deviant" Lapp population in Northern Norway (Hoem 1976).

We will not by this conclude that variations in culture and in patterns of preference between various social classes or communities are irrelevant for educational attainment. But none of them is of constant strength. - It therefore is remarkable that the parents' education effects demonstrated in the thirteen nations-study (- by the authors termed: "cultural capital") has been that stable over a long period. - But one should expect that differences in culture and patterns of preference between different strata with some mutual contact, i subject to processes of diffusion, so that the differences in the long run will diminish.

The school attainments of some immigrant groups may also be interpreted from a different perspective: collective survival of communities within a foreign context. Some immigrant groups and communities in "peripheral" areas are strong in cohesion and group discipline; they perceive themselves as outsiders in relation to the society, consider themselves as foreigners within a society that is foreign to them. Education is the more open and calculable field of advancement in this society. "Positive" school behaviour then may serve a double strategy: it expresses obedience to a background family that retains internal discipline and solidarity; at the same time it is a mean for coping with a foreign social order.

The outcome of this interplay between cultures, solidarities and strategies will not necessarily be conflict-free assimilation to the "majority" culture and a learning content quite identical to that by "insiders"; the newcomers may experience tumbling-stones of the sort Bourdieu described. However, the single-mindedness and discipline reinforced by a well-integrated background milieu may compensate for such difficulties.

It is notable that school-teaching in most of this century was an occupational sector dominated by descendants of farmers or from and countryside teacher families (Aubert et al., 1955). The school to some extent was "converted" to their particular "orthodoxy". In some humanist disciplines these milieus even dominated at the university (Lindbekk 1962).

From a theoretical point of view, these examples processes might examplify a view of education as a Lebensgemeinschaft, according to the pedagogical theories of the Jena group (Stafseng 1996:114-125 and 289-293). One might conceive of the local community as a basis for committments and solidarities, that are continuous with those of the school or at least affirms them.

Such processes also might apply to some other "peripheral" categories than immigrant communities and areas where old Gemeinschaft feelings still are strong; as when modern women redefined their social roles and made educational advancement their highway from invisibility and serfdom to equal citizenship.

*****

In what ways did recent educational reforms feed into the various mechanisms here depicted? The current theories do not provide convincing explanations for the rather insignificant effects of the extensive as well as expensive reforms. - Did particular processes outside of the educational system work against the reform interests? - Particularly: have the families and local communities that formerly made schooling a main part of their strategies for upward social mobility, lost their motivating and disciplining force? - For the reason that these families and local communities themselves had been broken down by competing loyalties. One thus is confronted with two quite different perspectives on the educational process: one that emphasizes that the school represents modern differentiated, individualized and universalist culture; with some strata as insiders in relation to this culture; while others are subjected to a tough resocialization. - According to an alternative view, schooling is subjected to the strategies and disciplining forces of a number of competing subgroups, among them particularistic families, some of them capable of "colonizing" the school as well as some other segments of the modern Gesellschaft-society.

2

DESIGNS FOR A REFORM EPOCH

National policies for reconstruction and new development.

In our neighbouring countries, the post-war education reforms mainly related to the secondary school. The Norwegian reform process was more extensive: at first it consisted in a rebuilding of the primary school structure in the countryside. After that the reform interest turned to the lower secondary ("realskole") stage, then to upper secondary education ("gymnas") and higher education. The various reforms to some extent overlapped in time, but they may tended to «follow» particular cohorts. The reform cohorts in lower secondary school entered the upper secondary stage just in time to be the pioneers even there. They also were among the first to profit by the institutions for higher education that after 1970 were established in regions («districts») that had no university.

Another issue: the reform concepts underwent large changes in the course of the reform periods, so large that they rather should be considered *series* of quite reforms, joined by a common name (this especially relate to the changes at the compulsory stage). Therefore we must consider both the general traits of the «reform» at the individual school stage, and the changes in intentions, policies and administrative practices while the implementation of that reform took place.

At the outset we shall present the main reforms and initiatives the way they appeared within national politics.

Policies.

In 1945, the Norwegian political parties presented a common statement of political principles: *The Common Party Programme* ("Fellesprogrammet") for national reconstruction after the five years of war and German occupation. Here they stated:

> *"The school system must be coordinated so that all elements from the primary school to teaching on the highest levels interrelate in a natural way. This applies to practical as well as book-oriented forms of education. An advisory board for the school system as a whole should be established, subordinated to the Ministry of Education."*
>
> *Telhaug 1994:91*

The Government shortly after that appointed a commission for educational policies, *The Commission for Coordination.* In the course of the years from 1947 to 1952, this commission presented white papers for various parts of Norwegian education (notably: special education, continuation schools, teacher training, and administrative issues). Of special emphasis was that the rural schools must come on level with those in the cities. In its final statement (1952) the Coordination Commission went one step further: "Our competitiveness and independence as a nation largely depends upon our educational system (1952:16)": For that reason compulsory education must be extended; there should be an evening out of differences between (social) classes, and equalization of educational opportunities, particularly for the countryside (1952:15-16)

Even though they seldom were presented in great detail, these premises became recurrent during the period that followed. Mobilization of talent was emphasized by the two educational commissions that were appointed in 1965, to consider upper secondary education and higher education (Telhaug 1994: 140-141). One should promote social justice and reduce inequalities between geographical areas, social classes, genders as well as ethnic groups. From the 1952 statement of the Coordination Commission to the report in 1989 from a new commission on higher education (the "Hernes commission"), beliefs also were expressed that one would profit by more rational organization of the education system, more differentiated use of resources, better coordination between geographical areas, across institutional barriers, and between educational programmes.

However, during the first postwar period, the practical considerations of the authorities mainly related to the «backwardness» of the primary schools in rural areas. The rural schools were subordinated to regulations who allowed radical deviations from the standards and number of instruction hours demanded in urban municipalities. A policy of «consolidation» into larger schools, to be localized at more «central» places was considered to be a better solution from pedagogical as well as financial points of view.

In 1954, Stortinget established the agency that the Coordination Commission had asked for. The brief for the *Board for Educational Development* ("Forsøksrådet for skoleverket") provided it with wide-reaching authority; it might even dispense with current school acts and governmental regulations, in case this was considered to be "in the school's interest". During the next ten years this new body initiated a thorough restructuring of compulsory schooling both in organization and content. A new Folkeskole Act in 1959 authorized the individual municipalities to extend compulsory schooling from seven to eight or nine years, and a common set of regulations for urban and rural schools was adopted. In 1969, Stortinget decided that the principle of nine years of compulsory education should apply to all youth.

The Board's reform work at the lower secondary stage lasted beyond the mid-70s. Around 1970 the content of the reform was thoroughly revised. Now all municipalities had decided to introduce nine years of compulsory education according to someone or other organizational pattern.

In 1965, a new School Commission (later named the "Steen Committee" after its leader) was established to review upper secondary education. The Board previously had been in charge of the reform work even at this stage, but the new commission now took over this responsibility.

The 1965 School Commission presented its first report in 1967. It proposed that the "integrated" or "comprehensive" school concept should be extended from obligatory schooling to the next stage of the school system: all education at this stage should be integrated administratively, preferably even executed in schools that were common for all youth at that stage.

Because of disagreements about the name of the new school, the new Upper Secondary Education Act ("Lov om videregående utdanning") was not adopted by Stortinget until 1974; but in some counties planning for implementation of the new pattern started as early as 1970.

In 1965 a governmental committee also was established to consider the In Established in 1965 was even an commission to deal with the education at the *post-secondary* stage (it was termed the Ottosen Committee, after its chairman). Its work went parallel with that of the 1965 School Commission. The main recommendations of the committee for post-secondary education were presented in a (first) report in 1968. Worth noting is that the new upper secondary school, supposed to serve as the foundation for the new developments in higher education, still was in the planning phase, and rather large changes were even after 1970 introduced into the content and organization at the lower secondary stage.

Chapters 3-5 do not provide any extensive treatment of the higher education policies, and the empirical analyses in chapters 6 and 7 mainly employ the higher education development as a control factor. We, therefore, shall give some extra details relating to the development at this stage here.

In 1965, there were universities or «scientific colleges» judged to be on university level, in the counties of Oslo, Akershus, Hordaland and Sør-Trøndelag. The other areas were not completely devoid of higher education facilities. There were a number of colleges for the training of teachers, nurses and technicians and some other semi-professions. The students at these college level institutions then made up 20 percent of the higher education students in the country.

The Government now decided that a fourth university should be established within a city in one of the northern counties, Troms. This university was formally established in 1968.

In its first report (1968), the post-secondary school-committee recommended the establishing of "coordination centres" for higher education in all regions that had not universities. A new set of institutions, "district colleges", should be in charge of this function as well as develop university programmes (introductory level) and educational programmes in vocational and other subjects of local interest. This plan set the stage for several innovations during the next thirty years. Main intentions: evening out of regional inequalities, unification and more integrated use of the resources for higher education of each region. Also they should be bridges between the universities and the rest of the higher education field, and work for a «scientification» of academic life in the «districts».

The idea of district colleges with a large manifold of programmes, caught on. In 1992, 12 district colleges were at work, with altogether 19000 students (The first part of this development is presented in Kyvik 1980). Despite that the student numbers at the other colleges changed little, the «district counties'» proportion of higher education students now grew from 20 percent to 35 percent in the course of a few years

However, the functions of the district colleges became limited to that of providing particular educational programmes (more or less research-based). The coordination function was enthrusted to a new set of "county boards", mainly consisting of political representatives. The district colleges did not get any formal status ahead of the other colleges, and had to compete with them for resources.

Nevertheless, an important step had been taken to provide the «districts» with an equal share of post-secondary education. But any reform to encertain more "integrated use" of resources had so far not materialized. In 1991, the Government introduced a concept of «Network Norway», to ease such integration, but at first little was done to make this concept operative. More impact had a new (1993) *Higher Education Act,* who wiped out the administrative dividing lines between the individual colleges within each county. Regional coordination from now should be produced by intra-organization processes. This unification even related to the uses of the research resources of the district colleges. As important is that most counties by this time had established agencies for (applied) research, in close contact with the colleges.

Of less importance, at least in the short term, was that the universities and the colleges from 1993 were subordinated to one, common, *Higher Education Act,* who prescribed identical nomenclature for administrative bodies and divisions of authority. Some other, less noticed changes during the 1970 to 1990 period may have contributed more to the changes within the higher education sector: The teachers at colleges and universities got identical titles. This flagged a further «scientification» of the colleges. The main responsibilities of the colleges still related to semi-professional programmes and undergraduate courses in some university subjects. But around 1990, particular graduate programmes were introduced at some colleges (in petroleum engineering, business management and teacher training). Three colleges were even authorized to award doctor degrees.

Other reforms related to the grading system. College grades should count equal with university ("time for time principle") grades, and a common academic grade, «cand.mag», was established. As a result of all these innovations, the general conditions for educational mobilization were changed, within university areas as well as in the «districts».

The new organization of higher education was even in the 1980s and 1990s an unfinished project. However, the changes in ambitions and institutional structures were so manifold and wide-reaching that career impacts of the changes should be expected even among youth born after the 1960s.

*****

Table 2.1. Overview of Reforms and Policy Periods.

	Rural primary schools	Lower secondary reform	Upper secondary reform	Higher education policies
1945-57	First "consoli-dation" phase.	Reconstruction and new visions		
1957-67	Second "consoli-dation" phase	Period of "lined" lower secondary schools		Planning for larger student numbers
1968-75	Reinforced community schools: a common solution	Period of "integrated" lower secondary schools	Period of planning & prereform expansion	Period of "District" policies
1976-82	Continua-tion of former period	Routine developm. of new pattern	Reform period with varying reform concepts	District policies continued

Plans, Policies, Coordination.

The changes portrayed in this chapter, reached deeply as well as widely. The facilities of most local communities now were transformed, a unified, organization of higher education was forged at the national stage; and pedagogical tasks were redistributed between individual schools, school stages and regions.

A curious feature is that plans and designs for these reforms seldom were worked out on beforehand, to demonstrate how the entire new structure should function organizationally, financially or from the point of view of transmission of qualifications. This even was the case for the reforms on single school stages. The reason may be that the new institutions often turned out differently from what had been conceived even shortly before. Preconditions and objectives that were proclaimed decisive at the outset, vanished in the course of the reform, and other issues took their place. It is interesting that these changes of premises and developments seemingly were accepted with little uproar by politicians and public. After 1960, the former folkeskole-policies of economizing by means of «consolidation» gave way to decentralized as well as steadily more expensive developments. At the lower secondary stage, a differentiated, «tracked» - and to some extent worklife-oriented concept was succeeded by one emphasizing integration within the individual school, and contact in with local culture. The upper secondary school gave up its original intention to reduce the curricular distance between academic and vocational schooling, and it developed within the confines of more limited financial resources (particularly: smaller amounts of instruction time than was planned originally). The new higher education concept contained at first a clear hierarchy of institutions, but after 1980 it changed into one that minimized the differences between various kinds of "higher" institutions. The college sector even adopted a number of programmes who formerly belonged to the secondary stage.

The analysis of reform *outcomes* for these reasons, therefore, must consider that the reforms in some cases appeared in versions that differed between periods and between counties and municipalities. The presentation in the next chapters, therefore, can not be limited to the main intentions among politicians; it also must cover the changes in administrative routines, finances etc during a longer period, during which the content of the reform sometimes changed radically.

Data, variables, methods.

The data used in the empirical analyses below, relate to: 1. Individual educational attainments (dependent variable), 2.Individual background data, and 3. Educational regimes of particular municipalities and counties (causal variables).

The data on individual backgrounds were gathered from the census informations (relating to the parents) in 1970 and 1980. They relate to the parents' informations on their occupations, levels of education, home locality and family compositions. The parents' occupations were classified by Goldthorpe's (1980) 7 classes scale (see Gooderham et al. 1993). In our analysis these classes were collapsed into: Professional (Goldthorpe classes I and II), Intermediate stratum (classes III, IV and V) and Manual work (classes VI and VII). The parents' levels of education were classified: nothing but compulsory = 0, "realskole" or other short secondary education = 1, completion of upper secondary education (gymnas exam level) = 2, short higher education = 3, higher education, graduate level= 4. Most of our analyses added the scores of the two parents to a sum score varying from 0 to 6 (sum scores 6, 7 or 8 then were given = 6). On the home locality variable, we separated between dispersed areas (=communities with less than 200 individuals) and densely populated areas (sometimes we also separate·between large cities (the four largest) and other densely populated areas.

The educational *regimes* were classified on the municipal level (compulsory and lower secondary education) as well as for individual counties (upper secondary and higher education). For these classifications several sources were used, chiefly: The Governments information periodical *Norsk skole* *(1957-1983), Skolens årbok (1967-1971) NOS Educational Statistics,* Ingebrigtsen 1977. Kyvik 1980, and the Government's 1984 White paper on higher education.

Our main variable is *educational attainment.* This is understood as: level of highest completed educational programme (or percentages with grade from upper secondary education or from higher education). This impact variable is the one that is most directly influenced by the reforms (and more valid and reliable than the testscores or distributions of grades within some or other educational programme). But this also is the most relevant indicator of educational attainments as intervening variables between schooling and succeeding career (See Listhaug et al 1982).

The various educational programmes are scored according to the classification of programmes that was developed by the Norwegian Office of Statistics (Statistisk sentralbyrå). Here each individual programme was located within a scale from 1 to 20, that represent the minimum number of school years considered necessary for completion of that programme (reckoned from the fi:rst year in primary school). Completed primary school is scored 6. Completed prereform obligatory school ("folkeskole") = 7, completed postreform, lower secondary "youth school" = 9 .). Completion of a voluntary tenth year in lower comprehensive secondary school was scored =10. Completed third year in upper secondary education ("gymnas" level exam) =12, lowest university exams ("examen philosoficum", "grunn-fag" exam, or first year of semi-professional school) = 13, etc. Voluntary continuation school ("framhaldsskole" or "folkehøgskole") after prereform (7 years) compulsory school is scored = 8.

Because of the "upgrading" of a number of educational programmes between 1975 and 1982, our analysis focus the attainment changes between 1982 and 1992, where classification patterns were constant. After 1980, this file was supplemented with data from the yearly reports on registred students and on completed educational programmes from Norwegian educational institutions. From the Norwegian Student Finance Authority (Statens lånekasse for utdanning) parallel data for Norwegian students abroad were added.

The material consist of a 7 per cent sample of the populations born 1954 to 1973, altogether 105.000 individuals, who lived in Norway in 1992.

Chapters 3-5 treat the reform effects separately for each stage: the effects of the "consolidation" reform, those of the introduction of compulsory nine-year lower secondary education, and that of the "new" upper secondary school. Chapters 6-7 study the combined attainment impacts of these reforms plus those of the "district" policies in higher education.

Our "dependent" criterion mainly is to what educational level did the various populations advance ("average attainment level"). This measure sometimes is supplemented with : proportion (percentage) who attained an upper secondary grade. Other places, it is supplemented by, the proportion (percentage) who completed some higher education programme.

*****

3

«CONSOLIDATION» IN THE COUNTRYSIDE

Main issues in this chapter are: if the small, undifferentiated primary schools in the countryside were inferior to «ordinary» schools (meaning schools with age-homogeneous classes), and the attainment changes by «consolidation».

Policies.

Compulsory education was regulated by the two Primary School Acts of 1936, one for the folkeskoler in cities and one for folkeskoler in rural municipalities. The city school was based upon the conception of a differentiated organization with separate classes for each birth cohort, while the main premise for the rural school rather was that of flexible adaptation to the practical conditions of a geographically dispersed population, that was not able to send children to school six days a weak, all through the 39 school weeks of a year.

In most of the rural municipalities a three days- a- week model had been adopted. This was preferred for several reasons: one single schoolroom could in the course of the week house two classes. Thus, the expenses for heating, cleaning and general uphold could be kept low. The three-day school also made for a clear division of responsibilities between home and school (three schooldays, four home-days a week), and limited the school transports needed..

These organization patterns were within the regulations lain down in current School Acts. According to Primary School Acts of 1936, the minimum amount of instruction hours in rural areas was 4500 (sum for seven years in compulsory school), against 6400 in the cities.

In 1950, half the schools in rural municipalities had just one or two school classes (see table 3.1). This commonly implied teaching of three or more birth cohorts in common class. A smaller number of instruction hours (two thirds of that in an urban school class) must cover (= be divided between) pupils at very different levels in their learning career. However, the total number of pupils at these schools was not large. In 1948, they made up one sixth of all pupils in rural municipalities. A larger number - 50 percent – attended fully divided schools (and one third were at schools between these two "ekstreme" models.

The conditions in rural schools were aggravated by a permanent shortage of trained teachers. In 1955, 21 per cent of the primary school teachers had not a certificate from a teacher's college. Most or these also had not even a grade from upper secondary school (NOS, School Statistics 1954-55:23). Some of the smaller school had not at any time during the 1950s had a (formally) qualified teacher. In two thirds of the municipalities there was no teaching of English, mostly for the reason that no teacher with the relevant qualifications was at hand in any of the schools of the municipality. Also, many school buildings were old (often dating back to the first decade of the century). In 1954 only 8 per cent of the countryside schools had a room for physical exercises; even fewer had a school kitchen. For carpentry the conditions were better; 30 per cent of the rural schools had a special room for such activities (NOS: School Statistics 1954-55).

The Labour party, then and for the next twenty years Norway's governing party, stated in its very first postwar election programme (1945) that it wanted to:

> "strengthen the rural school by gathering the pupils at larger and better equipped schools on central places».   Telhaug 1994:263

The Commission for Coordination carried this intention further: it said that the small schools made up a very unfortunate situation (Samordnings-nemnda, VI, 1948:11 and 16). In the current debate, there was particular emphasis on lacking facilities for physical exercises, handicrafts and school kitchen (important subjects according to the 1936 Act). Improvements of buildings and other facilities was considered crucial both for adequate teaching and recruitment of qualified staff (Sirevåg 1979:202-205, Karlsen 1993:111).

In a white paper (1954) devoted to the general improvement of school conditions (postwar reconstructions now had advanced so far that one could present ambitions above those of a return to prewar standards) the Government stated that an equalization of conditions between city and countryside should be established. The next year it abolished the three-days-per-week option. The municipalities were instructed to introduce five-days-a-week schooling in the course of the next four years.

The 1959 Folkeskole Act laid down a general principle of six schooldays a week. The number of school weeks per year should be 39 irrespective of locality (Rust 1989:213.). The 1959 Act also presented a demand that the municipalities should have specialized school administrations: in each municipality, there should be a school-committee, appointed by the municipal government, a local headmaster's conference, and a municipal "school inspector", responsible for current affairs of the school sector as well as the general uphold of educational quality (Rust 1989:214).

The 1954 white paper signalled a break in the rural school policies. It was succeeded by new requirements relating to curricular demands, instruction hours, local administrative conditions, and national financial provisions, some of them already mentioned, others to be lined out below. Because of these changes, the conditions and developments after the mid50s should be considered separate from those of the first postwar period. It must be assumed that both the local policies related to "consolidation", and the school-internal (pedagogical) and other effects of the Government's policies differed between the two periods.

The small countryside schools of the early 1950s were usually badly equipped, and the pupils had fewer hours of instruction than those in larger schools. However, because the number of pupils per school and per teacher was small, the expenses per pupil were larger than in fully divided schools (see Table 3.1). For these reasons. a more "centralized" model, was asumed to improve both educational quality and municipal finances.

The view that a reorganization should take place was hardly contested. In Stortinget, some politicians from the Farmers' party expressed reservations against a centralizing of local schools, and most parliamentarians were of the opinion that "consolidation" should not take place if municipal authorities were against. The (later) professor of pedagogics, Martin Strømnes, in 1947 published an energetic pamphlet against the current changes in the school organization of the countryside. He argued that a situation with pupils of different ages working together was fortunate from a learning point of view. However, the book evoked little interest.

*****

A survey of educational levels among soldiers in 1949 (Coucheron Thrane 1953) showed that the number with education beyond the compulsory minimum, was much smaller among men from rural municipalitities than among men from urban backgrounds (55 per cent against 29 per cent). This confirmed the impression that the educational system in the countryside was backward. A government survey of municipal school boards members showed that most of them wanted schools with more age-homogenous classes than currently. But a large minority was against "sending small children to larger schools" - which usually meant: schools farther away (Stortingsmelding nr. 9, 1954, Telhaug 1984:264). This indicated a widespread support for "consolidation" of the primary school system in this period; but also some - latent - opposition against carrying this development too far.

Demographic considerations added force to the view that there should be a centralization of compulsory education in the countryside. Recent birth cohorts (the »postwar baby boom») had increased by about thirty per cent. From 1955 these cohorts would enter school and produce increasing pressures on capacities. These pressures would come on top of the foreseen demands to increase the amount of instruction time per week. Some places this demand could be met by minor enlargements of existing school buildings. But in most outlying areas the conditions were more critical. The schools not only were small, they also lacked «modern facilities» like school kitchens. And many school buildings were old, dating back to the first decade of the century, and one would have to build entirely new schools. But how viable were the more peripheral communities, with no chances for industrial development ?

The Government's 1955 demands implied a large step towards equality between rural and urban areas. In rural areas the minimum instruction time should increase by two thirds, following the new demands. This would expand the school expenses by a similar amount.

On the other hand, the Government claimed that the improvement of (rural) school conditions should be a governmental responsibility. And the financial support to the municipalities ("ear-marked" for school purposes) was stepped up. During the 1960s, 25 to 85 per cent of the current expenses (i.e. of the expenses considered «normal» for a school with a particular number of classes and pupils) were covered by the government. Most rural municipalities were allocated to the 85 percent category. From the point of view of the municipalities, the most serious obstacle for an educational upgrading (and at the same time preserving a decentralized school pattern As well) now seemed removed, even in municipalities with very strained budgets.

But now also a quite new issue appeared in municipal school politics. Most of the rural municipalities had no facilities for secondary schooling within their borders, and the conditions were commonly no better in neigbouring municipalities. Where should the facilities for extended compulsory schooling be located? - Mainly at the municipalities who already had selective lower secondary schools («realskoler»)? At first this question of localization appeared to be a theoretical issue of small common interest, but gradually it became clear that local school politics from now primarily must be to participation in the planning and considerations for the new lower secondary school pattern. This issue was not only important for the educational prospects for local youth. As important were the direct and indirect implications foreseen for the municipal finances.

The Board for Educational development as early as 1955 stated that the municipalities' participation in the planning for the new lower secondary school was conditional upon their

> *«reorganization of the local school structure by the closing of smaller schools» ... and*
> *«general involvement in local educational development, and general committment to*
> *the educational development envisaged by the Coordination Commission»*
> *Norsk skole 1955/2-3:3-6.*

These principles were repeated on numerous occasions (Norsk skole 1958:104-107 and 1959:173). Even in the early 1960s the main issue in local school policy was who should host the new school facilities (and who would be the loosers in this game) and the general preparations for a new situation with extended schooling.

But around 1965 some quite new options appeared, who reflected that quite new conceptions of lower secondary schooling were emerging. They crystallized into the idea that there should be lower secondary schools in all municipalities, even the very small ones (in so far as this could be arranged practically). Within the most «peripheral» municipalities' there even developed demand that all main parts of the individual municipality should have its own secondary school.

Institutional developments.

Table 3.1 gives an overview of the school development in rural areas 1946 to 1964. During the early postwar period (1946 to 1954) the number of primary schools in rural areas decreased by about 40 a year. The schools with two classes accounted for most of this reductions. 350 such schools vanished, they during the period, most of them because they were closed. Some places this development was experienced as dramatic, but in the light of later developments, the amount of «consolidation» was moderate, despite the strained conditions of municipal finances shortly after the war. The closing of schools did not amount to more than one percent per year.

Table 3.1 . Number of Primary Schools («folkeskoler») in Rural Municipalities 1946 - 1964.   By School pattern.

	1946-47	1949-50	1954-55	1964-65
Undivided	819	796	649	326
2 classes	2256	2159	1900	805
3 classes	877	813	729	487
4 classes	915	930	915	613
5 classes	130	134	177	174
6-7classes	486	493	699	830
Sum	5483	5325	5069	3235

From. NOS: School statistics for 1946-47, 1949-50 1954-55 and 1964-65.

Did the new political situation after 1955 - when the Government demanded upgrading – who mostly should be payed for by the Government, produce a slowing down of the consolidation process? The clear conclusion from table 3.1 is no. During the ten years from 1954 to 1964 , altogether 1800 rural

Table 3.2. Current Expenses per Pupil (NKR, nominal value) in Rural Schools. 1951-55 by Number of Classes per School.

	"Un- divide d"	2 clas- ses	3 clas- ses	4 clas- ses	5 clas- ses	6 clas- ses	7 clas- ses	Sum
1951-2	790	656	581	526	489	502	566	592
1954-5	945	774	674	602	571	585	635	651

From: NOS. Skolestatistikk 1954-55, p.27.

Table 3.3. Current Expenses per Pupil (NKR, nominal value) of Primary school (rural and urban) 1969-70. By number of students per school.

	Be- low 13	13 - 30	31 - 50	51 - 85	86 - 90	91 - 150	151- 200	201 - 350	351- 500
Sum	4790	3890	3540	3331	3221	2901	2462	2418	2197
Of this: teachers' wages	3051	2283	2089	1989	1887	1657	1473	1523	1431

From: Driftsutgifter i de kommunale grunnskoler regnskapsåret 1969. Kirke og undervisningsdepartementetn, Oslo, notat 5/4 1971, p.7.

schools vanished. Which each year makes up 3 to 4 per cent of the remaining schools. In the course of the period as a whole, the number of schools with just one or two classes was halved. The number of 3 and 4-class schools decreased as well.

Parallel to this, there was a steep increase in the number of pupils who had daily (publicly organized and financed) transport from home to school, from 7 per cent of all primary school pupils to around 20 per cent.

Because that the municipal borders were redrawn around 1965, comparable statistics for the rest of the 1960s is not available. But within the country as a whole, the total number of primary schools now decreased by about 40 each year, equalling one percent of the total numbers. It now mostly was a question of closing schools with two or four classes. Most of the closures probably were in the rural areas. Implication: after 1955, the «consolidation» process continued, even speeded up, despite the new financial perspectives for schooling at this stage. The climax came just after the Stortinget (1959) had decided that compulsory schooling should be extended to nine years.

Resources in small and «normal» primary schools.

Were the larger, «fully-divided» (usually: more «centrally» localized) primary schools more favourable from the point of view of educational attainments (in comparison with smaller schools, who had two or more birth cohorts in each class?)

The answer to this question may depend upon what period is chosen for assessment. During the first wave of «consolidation» - around 1950 - it is a question of comparing two sets of rural schools, both of them with just two thirds the instruction time of that in urban schools. It was a period of austerity. However, the expenses per pupil in the smallest schools on average exceeded those in fully divided rural schools by about twenty percent, to compensate for equipment handicap and difficulties by teaching different age groups within common class.

The consolidation of the 1960s took place within a much more promising resource perspectives. The instruction time now was identical in urban and rural areas, and the remaining small schools were clearly the more advantaged from an expenses per pupil point of view (in schools with less than 30 pupils they on average exceeded those in schools with 150 pupils by more than 50 percent). The small schools by this became able to establish age-homogeneous groups in important school subjects. We also may assume that their ability to attract qualified teachers had improved, and that their equipment became as adequate as that in other schools. Most of the small «local» schools now resided in new buildings, buildings who commonly also provided various services for the surrounding community.

Attainments in the "old" community school

Were the small countryside schools of the early postwar period pedagogically inferior to the (larger) schools (mainly in more densely populated areas) with age-homogenous classes? An immediate impression would suggest a yes.

An early attempt to measure the school attainments of pupils from various types of countryside schools was carried out by Mogstad (1958). He studied the grades at stage 7, in mathematics and Norwegian language. The exams were organized commonly for the county as a whole; the grades, therefore, gave a valid impression of shortterm knowledge effects by the various schools. Mogstad studied the school protocols for 1949 and 1950 in 12 rural municipalities (some of them on the western coast area, the others in the eastern inland region).

Mogstads findings were unequivocal: in neither of the two subjects were the students from larger schools ahead of those from schools with just one or two classes. To the extent that attainment differences appeared at all, they were in favour of the smaller schools. These data did not correct for occupational composition of the various communities, but there is no reason to assume that the pupils from more peripheral areas had more favourable backgrounds as regards parents' levels of education etc.

Lindbekk (1979) studied the stage 7 grades (same subjects as Mogstad) of the 1940 birth cohort in ten rural municipalities (1965 borders) in Northern Norway who had maintained decentralized primary school patterns 1945 to 1955 (average number of pupils per school had increased from 27 to 30 during this period). They were compared with the grades in five municipalities who had "consolidated" during that period (average change in number of pupils per school by that increased from 28 to 60). In the municipalities with decentralized regime, the average expense per student was 10 per cent higher than in the municipalities with a centralized regime but it differed little from that in the nation as a whole.

The attainments were even studied by help of the 1956 to 1960 records at the National Board for Secondary Education ("Gymnasrådet"), who was in charge of the upper and lower secondary exams these years, and the files of the military conscription authority for Northern Norway were investigated, relating to the men who were enlisted for military service 1959 to 1964 (75 per cent of the men who belonged to the 1940 cohort, were found in these files). The attainment variables, thus, were more manysided than in the Mogstad study; they covered even educational careers until six years after leaving the folkeskole. The pupils were classified by the municipalities not by the school of the individual student. The data for this reason show the attainment differences between local school regimes rather than by individual schools. By this procedure, the attainment differences between the various school types schools may have been underestimated.

Table 3.4. Educational Attainments in the mid50s. By the Muni-cipality's Primary School Regime..

	Stable (decentralized) regime 1945-1955	Consolidated regime 1945-55
Pupils per school 1945-and 1955 Pupils per fulltime teacher 1945 and 1953	27.8-> 30.9 36 -> 38	28.6 --> 60.8 44 -> 31
Current expense per pupil 1953	NKR 696	NKR 599
Of all men born 1940 who entered the military: Average grades at stage 7 Per cent with vocational education Average testclass (age 20)	5.3 (N=159) 17.0 (N=167) 4.8 (N=167)	5.4 (84) 17.3 (120) 4.1 (248)

Of all men born 1940:
  Percent with realskole grade.
 	
Of all men and women born
  1939-42: Gymn. grade percent
	7.0 (N=251)
	
	4.0 (N=2008)
		6.4 (N=156)
		
		4.1 (N=1248)

Source: Samfunnsendring, 1979:.122,133,136,140

The conclusion from this study, shown in table 3.4, nevertheless is clear. The attainments were almost identical by the two regimes. This parity of outcomes included the· stage 7 grades. The percentage who attained some vocational education was a little larger in the consolidated municipalities, the average test scores and the percentage who had completed an «academic» lower secondary grade («realskole»), were a little higher in «unconsolidated» municipalities.

Two of the decentralized and two of the «consolidated» and centralizing municipalities had lower secondary schools («realskoler») within their borders.   It is interesting that the attainment data just showed small effects of this additional facility.

In table 3.4, the impact of the pupils' individual backgrounds were not considered. After the children og professionals, business men and

functionaries had been taken out of the calculations, the attainments decreased a little, but the pattern between municipalities did not change.
The data from the two studied, therefore, support that the two regime types were on equal level in school attainments. This was the case within a short term perspective, limited to primary school grades, as well as in relation to some more longterm indicators.

Attainments in the "new" community school..

The introduction of the new, compulsory, nine-year school extended over a long period. Even in the school-year 1968-69, when the 1954 cohort was on stage 9, youth from 141 municipalities was exempt from the new principle. 126 of these municipalities were in the countryside. In two thirds of them, voluntarity of education beyond seven years even applied to the next age group, that born in 1955.

Table 3.5. Attainments until age 36 or 37, as a function of Primary School Regime. 1954-55 cohort.

	Decentral regime maintained 1955- 66	Consolidated before 1966
Number of munic.(1965)	50	17
Average number of students per school N=	25.6 322	123.3 499
Average attainment levels at age 36	11.43 SD= 2.45	11.04 SD=2.41
Per cent with: Upp. sec.grad High.ed.exam-	38.6 22.9	36.7 10.2
Per cent with: no education beyond compulsory school	12.5	14.7

The municipalities who were "survivors" from the ancient lower secondary regime, differed in various ways. Of special interest are those with small primary schools even in 1968, or just had implemented a large-school principles quite recently. In 50 of these (rural) municipalities, the average number of classes per school was below 3.5. Main practice here was schools with two or more age groups in each class. In 17 (rural) municipalities, the average class number per school was 7.0 or larger. Here, the principle of age-homogeneous classes clearly prevailed. In eleven of these municipalities, the average school size had doubled in the course of the last ten years.

Table 3.5 sums up our data on attainment development up to age 36-37 (1992) for youth born 1954 and 1955 in these 67 municipalities, altogether 771 individuals. We have no data on school grades, but the material on educational careers is complete even for higher education grades.

The main story of Table 3.5 is easily told. It no longer is a question of attainment parity between the two regimes: the youth from municipalities who maintained dispersed primary school patterns, were ahead of the others (most of whom had consolidated recently) on four out of five criteria. Their advantage was especially clear in average attainment levels. The attainment level difference between the two regimes averaged 0.4 , which is statistically significant (the other differences were too small to be significant on .05 level).

It is interesting that more of the upper secondary graduates from «unconsolidated» than from «consolidated» municipalities completed programmes in higher education (46 per cent against 33 per cent) at stage 14 or higher. Even this difference is statistically significant on .05 level).

About half the municipalities surveyed had at that time selective lower secondary schools ("realskoler") within their borders. This condition had some attainment effects, which we shall return to in the next chapter. Suffice it to say that the attainment differences between consolidated and unconsolidated regimes were not due to the differences in access to a local secondary facilities.

The regression analysis reported in table 3,6 considers both the primary school patterns, lower secondary conditions in the municipalities and individual background factors. Reference category for the regression coefficients was: there was no selective lower secondary school (realskole) within the municipality. The background factors, had these reference categories: for women: men, for professional class background and working class background: "other backgrounds"; for parents' (combined) level of education: no education beyond compulsory,

Table 3.6. Attainment Impacts of Individual Back-
ground. By Primary School Pattern. 1954-55
cohort in municipalities witj "old" primary school
pattern.(OLS)regression coefficients.

	Regr.coeff.: attainment level	*Regr.coeff.: Up. sec.grades percentage*
Constant effect of individual backgr. factors:		
- women	*-.0.64s*	*-14,3s*
- parents' educ.	*0.55s*	*0.8s*
- professional class backgr.	*0.95*	*17.5*
- working class background	*- 0.44*	*-7.5*
General effect of:		
- realskole in municipality	*0.19*	*4.3*
- "consolidated" primary school regime	*-0.05*	*-9.4*
Interactions of "consolid." regime with:		
- women	*-0.20*	*-2.0*
- parents' educ.	*-0.37s*	*-0.5*
- professional class backgr.	*0.82*	*8.9*
- working class background	*0.17*	*3.7*
Constant factor	*11.03*	*38.7*

s= Statistically sign.effect on .05 level.

The upper part of the table presents the general effects of the individual background factors: the gender difference in attainments amounted to 0.64 years in attainment levels, 14.3 in gymnas grades percent. Each step of education (=two years beyond obligatory, combined for the parents) added 0.55 in attainment levels, 0.8 in gymnas grade. The class difference (professional class minus working class, net of the other factors) amounted to 1.39 years in attainment levels and 25 per cent in gymnas grade rates.

The next section of the table shows that "consolidation" was associated with almost no attainment level effect, but a 9.4 per cent reduction in gymnas grade rates. These figures should not be interpreted as showing average attainment effects by various primary school regimes; they relate to the effects by reference category conditions (= by men, for parents education: just obligatory, for "other" class backgroundn pwofessional and working class).

How did the individual factors: social class, parents' education, gender and home locality - interact with the" consolidation factors? One might hypothesize that the more "modern" and "differentiated" regime evened out differences. - Within the larger (and maybe more competitive) milieu, more particularistic forces broke down; each individual is more free to choose his/her one's own future.

The bottom section of the table shows some redistributional effects by consolidation: a (statistically not significant) increase in gender differences in attainment, a (significant) decrease in the impacts of parents' education, and a (not significant) increase in class impacts (consolidation was associated with attainment increases for professional class background as well as working class background in comparison with "other" backgrounds", but that for professional background was larger).

Consolidation reappraised.

Data from two previous studies (related to the impacts of various primary school regimes in the early 1950s) showed that the inferiority of decentralized schooling was gravely overstated in the debate on educational policies in that period. This related both to the shortterm effects on attainments (grades) and attainments in a more longterm perspective.

Data relating to the conditions in the mid-60s confirmed this picture and showed even some attainment plus for the unconsolidated area. This superiority was especially clear relating to average attainment level. But even more suggestive was that it even related to attainments in higher education. But because of the generous extra resources to small countryside schools in the 1960s, we are not able to tell if the superiority was due to the school pattern itself or the resources.

The schools with just one to four classes were not distributed randomly between counties and geographical regions. - To what extent did their attainment plus reflect regime differences on higher stages? These differences did not vanish after the secondary and higher education regimes had been entered into the attainment analysis (see the table in Appendix II). It also is a question if they did survive the introduction of compulsory lower secondary comprehensive school and the (expensive) facilities associated with this schooling. Table 6.3 considers the attainments of the 1954-55 cohort as well those within the cohort born 1964-65, where the various primary school patterns interacted with the "youth school"as well as the «new» upper secondary school and the new «district» policies in higher education. Did the advantages by the "dispersed" primary schools remain? Appearing now is a more complex attainment outcome than the ones in tables 3.5 and 3.6. The attainment advantage of youth from «unconsolidated» municipalities remained in attainment *levels* (maybe they even increased) , but those relating to *higher education* vanished.

The results presented in this chapter are ambiguous in relation to the issue how much the extra *resources* counted for the attainments in the small primary schools of the 1960s. But the disadvantages by less differentiated input factors (in: composition of school classes, access to specialized teaching equipment, service by fully qualified teachers in all subjects etc.) clearly were compensated for by these "extras".

We may assume that the small school areas considered in tables 3.5 and 3.6 are representative for Norway's social and geographic "periphery" and the cultures of such areas. The data do not favour assumptions that a *conflict* reigns between the local cultures of such areas and the school's "middle class" culture. A Bourdieu'ian habitus-theory might well be reconciled with the attainment parity of youth from this periphery , but it should not remain when youth from this part of the periphery meet the challenges in higher education. The Jena-group's emphasis on conditions favouring «organic» communities inside the school and between local schools and their surrounding communities, may seem more relevant for the attainment outcomes we have presented. Maybe this counter-force explains why value conflicts and habitus factors (who much more focussed in the debate), had not the expected impacts.

*****

4

"YOUTH SCHOOL" REFORM

Main issues in this chapter are: How the new lower secondary school developed organizationally, and how the new regimes shaped the school career of youths from various backgrounds. – Did the effects of the «lined» school of the 1960s differ from those of the «integrated» school of the 1970s?

Lower secondary policies.

Around 1950, Norwegian youth after having finished an equal and common (except for the general differences between rural and urban schools) 7 year "folkeskole", one fourth of the cohort proceeded to a "realskole", that lasted two or three years. This school had a theoretical emphasis (though the third year - intended for youth who did not aim at the "gymnasium", was more "practical", and mainly intended for medium rank jobs in shops and offices). Another fourth of the cohort went to vocational programmes, mostly lasting one year (often just part-time education).

Most municipalities also provided "continuation" programmes, for youth who neither wanted realskole nor vocational schooling; the continuation programmes varied in content (in some municipalities they were vocationally oriented, other places more theoretical) and instruction time. But a large proportion of the cohort went directly into the job marked.

Half the lower secondary («realskole») graduates proceeded to an academic upper secondary school («gymnas») that lasted three years. Two thirds of the upper secondary graduates attended the university or a semi-professional college. The higher education number altogether made up ten percent of the cohort.

In its 1952 overview of the current educational situation, the Coordination Commission pointed our that Sweden and Great Britain now worked out plans for an extension of the compulsory education to nine years. Both these countries considered separate "lines" in the 9th school year. The Commission recommended that preparations should start for an obligatory, common, eight-years school, by the inclusion of the continuation school as a separate "line" alongside with the realskole. One member of the Commission advocated a more radical step: the establishing of a compulsory *nine-year* school.

Acting upon the recommendations of the Coordination Commission, the Government in 1954 proposed the establishing of a *Reform Agency*, charged with a continuous development of the educational system. A common, basic education up to ages 16-17 should be a main reference-point for its work (St.meld.9 1954:98-100). On the basis of scientific assessments, lines for academically as well as otherwise inclined youth should be developed (Slagstad 1994).

The Coordination Commission had in mind a school that brought together realskole and continuation school. While the academic line mostly should be identical to the well-established realskole, the Commission intended the "other" line (or lines) to be "richly varied".

Various arguments were presented for this development: Norway's competitiveness and independence as a nation is conditional upon an extension of compulsory education. A further point: this reform will reduce status- and class differences and further educational equality between urban and rural areas. The commission also produced some more pragmatic arguments: Around 1960 the small birth cohorts born in the mid-50s will enter the folkeskole. By introducing the reform in that period, one will not exceed the accustomed outlays for school purposes. The commission also believed that the future revision of municipal borders would create make more "rational" local school systems. Also, new educational methods will ease the problem of the "school tiredness" of 14 to 16 years olds (Coordination Commission 1952: 15-18).

Stortinget accepted these views. The newly established *Reform Agency* («Forsøksrådet for skoleverket») then singled out three municipalities for development work ("forsøk") with 9-year schools. The design reflected the

Coordination Commission's ideas: the realskole and a two-years continuation school shall be brought together under one roof and with one
common school principal. The second year of the continuation school shall
have general as well as vocational content, with an agricultural emphasis.
However, on one particular point the Reform Agency deviated from the
Coordination Commission's proposals: the development shall be conditional
upon that the municipality in question decides to extend extend compulsory
schooling to nine years.

In 1960 the Agency presented a new set of curricula for the more central
school subjects of the new school. There should be "lines", who differed
differed by their extent of severity. The school classes should be composed
on the basis of the curricula chosen, and the selection of students for the
various curricula should be based upon test scores, grades and the parents'
wishes.

However, when the issue was brought to Stortinget in 1961, critical views
were expressed: The politicians disliked the idea of early selection
according to ability, and objected to the establishing of organization models
that might determine the future careers of the students prematurely
(implication: within the current school system, more flexible careers were
possible than by the new model of the Reform Agency).

The Reform Agency in 1964 presented a revised plan. Streaming according
to talent should be limited to four subjects. (Only) in the 9'th year should the
pupils be allocated to classes on the basis of their curricula (streams). This
was a rather great change from the presuppositions presented five years
earlier, and the Agency went further by initiating a trying out of non-tracked
teaching in Norwegian all through the three years of the youth school.

Stortinget was even critical to the 1964 plan. The matter then was left
undecided, until the Government in 1971, following the recommendations
from a (new) committee for curriculum development in compulsory school,
abolished what remained of the principle of streaming or separate «lines».
There should be "individualized teaching" and "pedagogical differentiation"
instead of "organizational differentiation". The remaining demands for more
differentiated activities should be taken care of by subdividing the classes
(into not-permanent groups) in subjects considered particularly demanding
(Telhaug 1982). The principle of "lines" was by now definitely left aside.

The reason for this change of principles was not only that the idea of an early selection according to talent was unappealing (latent egalitarianism here may have joined hands with disbelief in psychological expertise); also, recent educational statistics had shown that the number of pupils who opted for the "academic" or most "demanding" lines/programmes steadily grew, and most schools gave in to the individual demands for "promotion" to more demanding lines (Norsk skole 1965/7). It therefore became difficult to present a clear model of the new school. One now was not able to estimate how many "other" classes "normally" would be needed for one gymnas-preparing class.

The presumption that the academic variant of lower secondary education should mirror the former (selective) realskole, also became undermined by new principles for entry to the upper secondary stage. The Government decided that lower secondary exam in just one foreign language should suffice for entry to the upper secondary stage (against previously two, of which German had proved to be a stumbling stone for many lower secondary pupils).

At first these new conditions caused small change. Despite that upper secondary intake now was made conditional upon qualifications in just *one* foreign language, the applicants who had just that, were excluded. The upper secondary school capacities were too small to allow intake of all applicants, and those with just one foreign language lost in the competition. But after the mid-70s, the lower secondary school lost this "disciplining" moment. Because of fast build-out, the upper secondary school became open for all who applied; no structuring premise for the content of lower secondary school could be found here. In the aftermath of these developments, even the rationale for «lines named vocational» vanished.

Institutional developments: Resources, school sizes, locations.

The decisions when and how the extension of compulsory schooling should be implemented, were produced within a complex interplay between the individual municipality, the Reform Board, and the Government (who mainly operated via its local representatives - the "school directors"). At issue was mainly: School locations, sizes, curricular emphasis, differentiation, and resources.

Central or "peripheral development/large or small schools?   In the early 1960s, the new, «extended», compulsory school was conceived as a «central» school. It had a number of lines, and catered for the demands of various types of pupils. One conceived of a large institution providing many specialized services.

In 1965, a non-socialist government took office. It appointed a new Reform Board, who adopted a decentralist profile. The main principle now became: «youth schools» in all municipalities. The authorities emphasized the manifold relations between the schools and their local communities, and the favourable social conditions in small-dimensioned schools. The new, small-dimensioned lower secondary school became the most visible aspect of an entirely new development in compulsory education.

In the early phase of the planning for a new lower secondary school, the Reform Agency considered four classes on each stage to be optimal, from financial as well as pedagogical points of view (Karlsen 1993:111-112). This view became the official policy of the Agency even in the 1960s. In the school year 1964-65, 43 per cent of the youth schools were even larger. They had five or more parallels (Norsk skole 1965/11:223). But for various practical reasons, "deviant" patterns had been accepted in 18 municipalities; they had just two (or one) classes per stage. The board that took office in 1965, eliminated the word "deviant" from the lower secondary school statistics. The number of small youth schools now grew very fast. In 1967-68, 201 schools had two or less parallels. 131 of the smaller lower secondary schools had 2 parallels/classes per stage, 59 just one. In 11 youth schools, the 7th and 8th graders made up just one (common) class (Norsk skole 1968/6:21, 27). The ideal of three or more parallels as the "normal" condition clearly was left behind.

But the new decentralist moods were not satisfied by making all municipalities self-sufficient in compulsory education. Some municipalities with very dispersed populations demanded even wider distributions of school facilities. According to the original plan, the Flakstad-Moskenes municipality should have one, common, youth school, to serve a birth cohort amounting to about one hundred. In 1975 this area had three youth schools. Another municipality - Lurøy - in 1975 had four youth schools, to cater for an even smaller birth cohort: about sixty

In Table 4.1 some main features of the lower secondary school development in Norway are lined out. The municipalities are ordered according to the year (autumn) of their first cohort in the 9'th year of compulsory schooling. Ten municipalities had their first nine graders as early as 1960. The «slowest» municipalities came not "in line" until fifteen years later.

The table shows how the average number of parallels per school sank in the course of the period; the reduction in school size was especially large among the 49 municipalities who had their first stage nine pupils in school year 1967-68. The table shows further reductions in school size among the municipalities who "reformed" after 1968. We also observe that by 1975-76, most of the early reformers had reorganized once more; they reduced their average number of parallels by one third.

Academic or practical emphasis? During the 1950s, the Reform Board invested much energy in the development of *alternatives* to the realskole-gymnas option inherited from the previous regime. The Board was especially impressed by the positive experiences with the programmes for agriculture, that some municipalities had developed for their new lower secondary schools (Norsk skole 1957:31). It conceived that each munici-pality should have its individual vocational programme, that was adapted to the local conditions. The 1958-plan for Lappish Karasjok, thus, had one line that combined agriculture, home economics and crafts, and one line for reindeer economics (Norsk skole 1959:173). But Stortinget's *no* to early selection for «academic» upper secondary schooling implied a no to «lines» as well. And the development work for vocationally oriented alternatives now stopped.

The secondary school that now emerged, therefore, retained its former goal: Prepare for (academic) upper secondary schooling, building on the practices of the old realskole. But to soften the matter, some minor «practical & aes-tetic»subjects were added to the curriculum, also a few school hours per week were reserved for "elective" issues. Instead of "lines", it now became a question of presenting more and less demanding versions of one common curriculum.

Alternatives to differentiation? The pedagogical challenge now became not just that to present realskole-issues for a broader selection of the youth; it was aggravated by new, ambitious, "integration" policies for handicapped youth: the state's 'special schools' from now retained just the most severely

Table 4.1 Municipalities by Year for the first
Lower Secondary School graduates (9th grade),
and Number of parallel classes per school.

Year of first pupils at stage 9	Munici- palities with first cohort that year	Parallels per school 1966- 67 (stage 7)	Parallels per school 1975-76 (stage 7)
1960-64	21	4.9	3.8
1965	34	4.2	3.4
1966	44	4.9	3.4
1967	49	3.6	2.9
1968	46	3.3	2.9
1969	55	3.9	3.0
1970	51	-	3.5
1971	46	-	3.2
1972	35	-	2.4
1973	30	-	2.6
1974	18	-	3.2
1975-1977	11	-	3.1

handicapped (Funksjonshemmede i samfunnet, 1977-78, Resultater og erfaringer, 1996-97). The main pattern should be: handicapped youth in "normal class". According to the calculations of the authorities, the former "special school-cases" in 1982 made up 1-2 per cent of the students in "ordinary" nine-year schools (Om grunnskolen, 1982:147), which implied: one (formerly classified as) "handicapped" youth in each third class. How were the practical problems by these "integrations" solved? For pupils with small ability and/or particularly lack of school motivation, most"youth schools" had established (small) "help classes". After "tracking" became disallowed, many municipalities (with doubtful legitimacy), introduced an option of partial exemption (of up to two school-days per week) from normal schooling. Instead of schooling, pupils might participate in work life (Telhaug 1982:253). After 1970 this solution was regularized by the authorities, and named "alternative education". About 10 percent of the 8th and 9th grade students participated in these "alternatives". Implication, just a minority of the pupils on "alternative" programmes came from the former "special school" category.

There also was an expansion of the supportive services within the individual school. In 1969-70, the expenses for "special instruction" made up 11 per cent of the schools' total wage expenses. In 1981-82 this proportion was 15.5 per cent (Om grunnskolen 1982:153), and altogether 10 percent of the pupils had such services (Om Grunnskolen 192:148-149) These resources to the individual school came on top of the resources by the «normal» formula. Schools with many pupils in need of such services, thus got significant additions to their resources.

The extraordinary, «supportive» teaching usually was carried out outside of the ordinary class context (Skog and Lund 1989:42), and the number with supportive teaching was close to the number who formerly had been allocated to the youth schools' "helping" classes.

In conclusion: The «lines» were succeeded by new routines for "diffe-rentiation". The new differentiation patterns were part-time, and differed from the preceding ways by not interfering with the rights to intake in upper secondary education.

Small schools, but how expensive? Each school, however small, now should serve the entire youth group. As was the case in the primary school, the Government covered the extra expenses considered necessary for securing "normal" quality in the smaller schools. The "ordinary" instructor-resource per "normal "youth school class per week was set at 47 1/2 hours (= 37 hours for "ordinary" teaching, the rest evenly divided between "special teaching" and more diverse activities, described as "development" and "social pedagogics" (Norsk skole 1972, 17: 83). When divided by the average number of students per class, this implies an average of 2.1-2.4 instructor hours per pupil, provided it had 3 parallels and full classes. In a school with 30 students on each stage (distributed between two classes), the teaching resource was 3.3 hours per student. In the smallest schools - the ones with just one class per grade and 20 students per class, the teaching resource was 3.9 hours per pupil. This equals 180 per cent of that in the first example.

These figures should be compared with the former "realskoler", where the instructor resource per class closely equalled the number of school hours for teaching: By 35 hours and a class with 25 students, the formula implied 1.4. In addition came some resources for the principal's administrative work.

Additional to these «normal» resources, the new lower secondary school got extra resources for development work, psychological help etc, from the Government's local representative, the school director.

The resources for the new lower secondary school were abundant, compared with the former system. And they crept upwards (*Om grunnskolen* 1982:149). From 1975 to 1981, the total instructor resource per pupil in compulsory education increased by 0.3 hours (this equalled 6 hours a week for a school class with 25 pupils).

However, despite the attempts to keep the lower secondary schooling within the home community, a few municipalities (altogether 15) had even in 1975 their lower secondary schooling otherswhere, because their populations were considered to be too small (for a youth school), or the internal communications of these municipalities were particularly bad. None of these municipalities were among the earliest youth school municipalities.

Table 4.2. Introduction of New Lower Secondary School. Reform Periods, Municipality types and School sizes.

Reform period	First Nine-graders	= birth year	Number of munic.	Of all towns (%)	Of all centr. rural (%)	Of all periph. rural (%)	Parallels per. sch. 1966	Parallels per sch. 1975
Pioneer	- 1966	- 1950	99	6	29	5	4.7	3.5
Early middle	1967-69	1951-53	150	50	30	43	3.6	2.9
Late middle	1970-73	1954-57	162	27	36	47	-	2.9
Late-comers	1974-	1958-	9	16	5	5	-	3.2
Sum N=			440 440	99 47	100 321	100 79	-	440

Two "new" regimes; similarities and contrasts.

The lower secondary schools of the 1970s differed much from those of the early 1960s. Common was nine years of compulsory schooling, and that the teaching should be within a common school building, with one, common principal in charge. But the differences were more numerous: They related to: 1). The internal organization of the school. A hierarchy of lines gave way to individualized teaching, combined with some new forms of tracking (relevant only for the least motivated and/or least abled ten per cent of the pupils). 2). Curricular principles (a system with academic as well as localist or vocational curricula) was succeeded by one common, mainly academically oriented curriculum, 3) School sizes (a pattern with rather large schools, was succeeded by one with large variation in class numbers and pupil numbers per school). 4) Local emphasis (in the first period: some lines with general and mainly academic focus, other lines with local focus; in the later period: schools for neighbourhoods, particulartly emphasizing the cultural content of the area).

Some other conditions could be added for the post 1970 schools: steady improvements of resources, (particularly relating to the supportive services), professional change: from staffs chiefly manned with teachers from the old realskole – most of them with university backgrounds - to staffs from teacher's colleges (mainly oriented towards the primary school); from schools with wide catchment areas, to schools for particular neigbourhoods; by that: schools with more internal homogeneity in culture and other pre-suppositions; while the cultural differences within the single school decreased, those between schools became larger.

Which of these moments were the more important for the attainment developments? One may argue that the early youth school regime presented a rather limited change from the previous system. The main change was: nine school years even for those who wanted no more schooling. - Did this create more widely spread school interests? Did a maturation effect occur among those who previously would have opted to leave? - Or was such maturations blocked by the internal homogenization of attitudes within lines, and mutual *antipaties* between lines?

The later version of the new lower secondary school was more integrated internally, on paper it was identical for all students in curricular content and teaching methods; and school-community relations were closer - at least at places with small youth schools. But the lower secondary schools of the second reform wave were probably more uneven in staff quali-fications. Because the schools had narrower catchment areas, the individual school was more homogenous in student composition, but the differences between schools were larger. - Maturing effects now developed without the cementing influences from lines. That might make for more equal developments of attitudes and interests within the individual school. - But the content of this "normalcy" varied more between schools

Attainment impacts of the "lined" school of the 1960s.

In the mid60s, four types of local regime were represented on the lower secondary stage: 1)"Reformed" municipality, with nine years of compulsory schooling, and a lower secondary school within the municipal territory, 2) Nine years of compulsory schooling, the last two or three years in a lower secondary school outside of the home municipality's territory. 3) Seven years of compulsory of schooling, followed by two or three years at a voluntary realskole within the home municipality. 4) Seven years of compulsory schooling. No secondary school within the municipality (but some vocational courses or "continuation courses" might be provided).

There also were some irregular cases: municipalities with compulsory nine years of schooling for one part of the municipality, just primary school with or without a local realskole for the rest (relevant example: in 1965 the municipality of Lyngen - one of the early youth. school reformers - "absorbed" parts of a neighbouring municipality that had not yet introduced the new system).

The attainment impacts by the introductions of lower secondary school system of the early 1960s have been treated in two previous studies. Gunvor Iversen (1969) studie a national material, relating to all men who entered military services in 1969 (=75 percent of the cohort). At that time they were 20 years old. Her main findings were that neither in urban nor rural areas did the lower secondary school reform produce changes in educational attainment averages or in the impacts of class backgrounds.

A more limited study of three early reforming rural municipalities in the Oslo-region (Lindbekk 1969) had a different outcome. The intakes in upper secondary school by the earliest post reform-cohorts in these municipalities were compared with those of the latest ante-reform cohorts. Shown here were rather large increases in upper secondary intakes (gymnas) and some diminishing of class background impacts.

In none of these studies were the individuals followed all through the upper secondary school («gymnas»); we therefore do not know who really completed the grade. The Iversen study did not include women, the Lindbekk study was limited to an area (municipalities surrounding Oslo) that clearly was not representative for the country as a whole.

Table 4.3 presents the school regimes relevant for the cohort born 1954. We observe that 73 per cent of the members of this cohort lived in municipalities with nine years of compulsory schooling for that particular cohort. 72 percent had a lower secondary "youth school" within the borders of their own municipality. The" reformed" municipalities made up 299 of all the 440 municipalities (3 municipalities with "irregular" solutions are not included in the figure). Among the reformed municipalities were all the largest cities: Oslo, Bergen and Trondheim. 27 per cent came from pre-reform municipalities

The "reformed" pupils of the 1954 cohort left primary school for stage 7 - lowest youth school stage - in 1967. In 1970, they finished youth school (stage 9). The stage 7 classes usually were quite heterogenous in abilities etc. At stage 8, some municipalities redistributed the pupils between tracks. Other schools just regrouped the pupils (between tracks) in the four most central school subjects, and postponed the composition of track-defined classes to stage 9. (These allocations were mainly on the basis of the individual pupil's combination of programmes ("kursplaner") in "tracked" subjects).

By this choice of cohort, the 1970 census data may be employed for the description of the pupils' individual backgrounds at age 16. Our first question (table 4.4) relates to the attainments until 1984 (=age 30). The 1984 classifications of programmes between stages were past the reclassifications of some higher education programmes (between secondary stage and higher education) that took place in the early 1980s, and make for comparability with 1990data.

Table 4.4 presents the average attainment levels and percentages who had completed upper secondary grades within age 30 (1984).

Table 4.3 1954-cohort by Lower Secondary Regimes Percentages.

	Lower sec.school within munici- pality	No sec. school within munici- pality	Per- cent of cohortl
Compulsory 9 year school	72	1	73
Pre-reform regime	17	10	27
Sum	89	11	100

Table 4.4. Attainments (until 1984) of the 1954 cohort. By Secondary Education Regime.

Site of lower second. school	Compulsory nine years	Not Reformed	Compulsory nine years	Not reformed
	Attainment level average	Attainment Lev. average	Upper sec. grades	Upper sec. grades
Within own municipality	11.49 SD=2.51	11.39 SD=2.35	39.7%	38.4%
Outside own municipality	10.81 SD=2,45	10.79 SD=2.28	25.0%	29.6%

Finding: the municipalities with no lower secondary school had much lower attainments than those with some lower secondary facitility (selective "realskole" or comprehensive "youth school") within their borders. The differences amounted to 0.6 in average attainment levels and 10 percent in upper secondary ("gymnas") grades. But the scores for the two lower secondary regimes were close; the comprehensive regimes were a little ahead in upper secondary grades, the selective regimes were a little ahead in average attainment level. Conclusion: Our initial assumption that the localization of facilities counted much for attainments, the organizational «model» little, is confirmed.

But the figures relating to attainment *distributions* present a more surprising picture: we observe that youths from the comprehensive municipalities were not more "equal" in outcomes than youths from selective municipalities. In comprehensive municipalities, the standard deviation for attainment levels was even a little larger than that in municipalities with selective lower secondary school. One explanation must be that nearly all the youth from municipalities with a selective school made use of this or some other secondary school facility. In the municipalities with no secondary facilities, the variations in attainment outcome were even smaller. Those with nothing but compulsory education dominated the distribution. Those who "broke out", made up just a minority.

Table 4.5. Educational Attainments 1984. By Regime and Individual Background. 1954 cohort.

	Compre-hensive regime	Selective regime	No sec. school in municip.
ATTAINMENT LEVELS			
Men	11.8	11.6	11.1
Women	11.2	11.0	10.6
Education background			
5-6	14.3	14.5	14.1
1-0	11.8	11.7	10.3
Social class background:			
Professional	13.2	12.9	12.3
Working class	10.9	10.8	10.3
Home locality:			
Densely popul. area	11.7	11.6	12.2
Dispersed popul.area	11.0	11.0	10.3
UPPER SEC.GRADES:			
Men	43.8	46.3	37.3
Women	35.1	31.0	21.2
Educational background			
5-6	78.7	81.0	75.0
.1-0	46.1	46.3	18.2
Social Class Background			
Professional	65.5	64.5	47.4
Working class	31.6	29.7	18.5
Home Locality:			
Densely populated area	43.2	43.4	36.9
Dispersed population area	32.2	32.1	18.4

In table 4.5, attainments are related to gender, locality, educational background and class – as well as by municipal regime. - Were the background impacts identical across regimes? The table shows some regime effects. While those of home locality and social class were much the same by the three regime types, differences appeared in the impacts of gender: to some extent the regimes also differed in impacts of educational background.

The average attainments of women from comprehensive municipalities were 0.6 years below the men's. This difference was equal to that in «selective» municipalities. It also was close to that in municipalities with no secondary school. - So far: no regime-generated difference But in upper secondary grade numbers, the gender impacts differed more between regimes. The difference was 16 percent by both the pre-reform regimes, but just half that in comprehensive municipalities.

The *educational background* impacts reviewed in table 4.5 were large: they amounted to 2,5 years (attainment levels) between high and low parent education levels (comprehensive regimes), against 2.8 years (selective regimes), and 3.8 years (municipalities who lacked secondary facilities). In upper secondary grades, the differences reflecting high and low parent educations amounted to 32.4, 34.7 and 56.8. In contrast to that, the effect *of social class* background was constant. This underlines that the background variables class and educational background represent different forces and processes, even when they are correlated, and that they must be applied separately in analyses.

Table 4.6 presents the outcomes from an (OLS)regression analysis, that included regimes, the four individual background factors from table 4.5, and interactions between regime and background factors. All the regime*background calculations have comprehensive regime as reference factors and show to what extent the background factor impacts by the "old" regimes differed from those after the reform.

For women (men as reference) negative coefficients appear by all four comparisons. This implies that the women pre-reform had lower attainment scores according to all the four prereform indicators. Implication: they generally *gained* by the regime change; they gained especially much in upper secondary grades, and by the change from selective to comprehensive regime. We also note that the attainment differences between dispersed and densely populated areas diminished by comprehensive regime.   Also, the

Table 4.5. Educational Attainments by Lower Secondary
Regime. Regime Effects on Individual Background Impacts.
(OLS)Regression Analysis of the 1954 cohort.

Regime- and Backgr. Factors	Attain.level	Up.sec.gr.
Women (men as ref.)	-0.15s	4.4s
Disp.home locality/(dense as ref.)	-0.18s	-2.8s
Parents'education (per 2 years)	0.75s	14.3s
Professional class		
(intermediate cl./no class as ref.)	0.22s	10.3s
Working class		
(intermediate cl/no cl.as ref.)	-0.43s	-5.2
Selective regime		
(Compr.h.reg as ref.)	-0.13	0.4
No sec.school		
(Compr.h.regime asref.)	-0.63s	-8.6s
Desentr.primary school		
(other prereform		
conditions in prim.ed as ref.)	-0.29s	5.8s
Interactions Regime*background effects:		
Women:		
by selective regime	-0.06	.-3.5
by nosec. Regime	-0.11	-0.6
Dispersed locality:		
by selective regime	-0.06	-0.5
by nosec. .regime	-0.20	1.0
Parents'education(per 2 years)		
by selective regime	0.06	0.8
by nosec. Regime	0.18	3.8
Professional class:		
by selective regime	-0.18	-3.6
by nosec. Regime	-0.48s	-14.1s
Working class:		
by selective regime	-0.05	3.5
by nosec. Regime	0.06	-5.8
Constant (=comprh.regime)	9.98	13.8

s.=statistically sign.effect (0.05 level).

Table 4.6 Educational Attainments by Lower Secondary Regime. Effects of Individual Background. (OLS) Regression analyses of 1954 cohort.

Regime- and Backgr. Factors	Attain.level	Up.sec.gr.
Women (men as ref.)	-0.15s	4.4s
Disp.home locality/(dense as ref.)	-0.18s	-2.8s
Parents'education (per 2 years)	0.75s	14.3s
Professional class (intermediate cl./no class as ref.)	0.22s	10.3s
Working class (intermediate cl/no cl.as ref.)	-0.43s	-5.2
Selective regime (Compr.h.reg as ref.)	-0.13	0.4
No sec.school (Compr.h.regime asref.)	-0.63s	-8.6s
Desentr.primary school (other prereform conditions in prim.ed as ref.)	-0.29s	5.8s
Interactions Regime*background effects:		
Women:		
by selective .regime	-0.06	.-3.5
by nosec. Regime	-0.11	-0.6
Dispersed locality:		
by selective regime	-0.06	-0.5
by nosec. .regime	-0.20	1.0
Parents'education(per 2 years)		
by selective regime	0.06	0.8
by nosec. Regime	0.18	3.8
Professional class:		
by selective regime	-0.18	-3.6
by nosec. Regime	-0.48s	-14.1s
Working class:		
by selective regime	-0.05	3.5
by nosec. Regime	0.06	-5.8
Constant (=comprh.regime)	9.98	13.8

s.=statistically sign.effect (0.05 level).

the impacts of educational background became smaller.

Common for these trends are: they present *diminishings* of background factor impacts, especially in relation to upper secondary grades. But the descendants from professional background *gained* by the reform (especially when they are compared with the pupils of pre-reform municipalities with no secondary facilities). At the same time, the impacts of the regime factor were inconsistent for working class pupils. In sum the attainment *difference* between the two classes appear to have widened after the regime change.

Impacts of the "integrated" comprehensive school of the 1970s.

About 150 municipalities had their first compulsory nine-year cohort at grade 7 later than 1967. 27 percent of the sample belonged to the "late" municipalities. For them, the "new" regime meant: lower secondary schooling within the borders of the municipality.

We now shall observe how the *regime changes* influenced attainment developments. These developments are considered: 1) Maintained compehensive regime (with a "youth"school within the home municipality), 2) From selective lower secondary regime (and a"realskole" within the home municipality) to comprehensive regime (and a "youth"school within the home municipality), and 3) From municipality with no secondary school) to a comprehensive regime (with "youth"school within the municipality). A few municipalities, with other types of regime, shall be left out of this analysis.

The analysis partly will consider the developments from the 1954 cohort (stage seven entry 1968) and the 1962-64 cohort (who entered stage seven 1976-1978). While the older cohort belonged to the period with "lines" or some remnant of "lines", the younger cohort belonged to the period past that. Attainments until age 30 (older cohort) and ages 28-30 = until 1992 (younger cohort) are compared.The background data, from the censuses 1970 and 1980 are not quite comparable, as they (older cohort) relate to age 16 against (later cohort) against ages 16-18 (younger cohort). Some calculations are also presented for the cohorts born 1954-55 and 1964-65, relating to attainments until age 27 (or 28). Here both the attainments and the background data were comparable, but the measurement reached shorter, and the number of pre-reform municipalities was smaller than i the former analysis.

Table 4.7 reviews the general attainment developments within the three regime categories: for the 1954 cohort and for that born 1962-64. Attainment gains appeared by all three categories of regime development, but the sizes of the gains differed: The ones in"stable" youth school municipalities and in municipalities who formerly had no secondary school, were close. Those in municipalities that formerly had selective regimes, were just half that large.

Both these trends were unexpected. For one, the municipalities who formerly had no secondary facilities, apparently got no "extra" by their entry into the club of more favoured municipalities (who had had their own lower secondary school even in the 1960s). The pre-reform attainment differences between these two groups of municipalities remained. Secondly: The former attainment equality between municipalities with selective and comprehensive regimes vanished after the reform. The reform apparently produced an *attainment decrease* for the municipalities that formerly were served by selective secondary schools.

Table 4.7. Effects of Regime Changes. Educational Attainments until Age 29, by Lower Secondary Regimes . From 1954 cohort to 1962-64 cohort.

Cohort/ School regime 1968	Upper sec.grades	Attainment level	Standard dev.(all.l)	N
1954 cohort				
Comprehensive 68	40.4	11.43	2.51	5051
Selective 68	39.4	11.44	2.35	1180
No secondary 68	29.1	10.75	2.28	673
1962-64 cohort:				
Comprehensive 68	54.7	11.75	1.95	10920
Selective 68	48.0	11.59	1.99	2510
No sec. sch.68	45.5	11.39	1.99	1505
Change :				
Compreh maintained.	+14.3	+0.32	-0.66	
Selective -> comprh.	+ 8.6	+0.15	-0.36	
No sec.sch->comprh.	+16.4	+0.35	-0.29	

We also observe that the largest reductions in *standard deviations* came in the municipalities who were comprehensive even in 1968. In other words: the transition to a comprehensive regime brought neither extra attainment increases nor smaller attainment variations.

We shall return to these matters in chapter 6, who treats these issues in the light of regime changes on other stages as well. We now turn to the ways the attainments were *distributed*.

In table 4.8, the changes between the two cohorts are studied by a simple comparison of the attainment differences between genders etc. . The changes in attainment differences are summed up in the column to the right in the table.

Table 4.9 presents the same material by means of (OLS)regression calculations. Reference factors in the regression analysis are: 1) For regime: comprehensive regime even in 1968, and 2) For individual background factors: Men, Densely populated home community, Parents with no education beyond compulsory, and: Other class background than Professional and Working class.,

The tables disclose some (diverging) changes in attainment distributions, associated with the various regime developments.

More than two thirds av the pupils belonged to municipalities with comprehensive regime in the 1960s as well as in the 1970s. We observe that in these municipalities, the women, and youth from dispersed locations gained (in relation to their reference categories), while the impact of educational background diminished. The class effect increased in upper secondary grades, but diminished in attainment levels. Most of these trends were statistically significant. Did the newcoming municipalities diverge from municipalities with more stable regimes?

First finding: the municipalities who previously had selective regimes or just primary schools, had extra upper secondary grade gains for women as well as for youth from dispersed home locations. In the municipalities that formerly had no secondary facilities, such gains also applied to average attainment levels. The regime change, therefore, produced extra attainment gains in favour of these groups.

But the educational background factor developed otherwise: Here impact *increases* by the regime change, and they were so large that they neutralized the diminishing of educational background impacts in "old" youth school municipalities. In other words: the regime change reaffirmed the impact of this factor.

Table 4.8. Educational attainments changes from the 1954-55 cohort to the 1964-65 cohort. By regime developments.

A.Attainment levels

Regime change 1968-76	1954-55 cohort			1964-65 cohort			Inequal. Reduced/ increased .- / +
	Men	Women	Diff	Men	Women	Diff	
Cpr.h>->cprh.	11.8	11.3	0.5	11.6	11.8	-0.2	-0.7
Selective>cprh	11.7	11.1	0.6	11.6	11.8	-0.2	-0.8
No.sec>cprh	11.1	10.7	0.4	11.3	11.8	-0.5	-0.9
	Dense	Disp.	Diff	Dense	Disp	Diff.	
Cprh>cprh	11.8	11.0	0.8	11.8	11.4	0.4	-0.4
Selective>cprh	11.7	11.0	0.7	11.8	11.4	0.4	-0.3
Nosec>cprh	11.3	10.8	0.5	11.6	11.5	0.1	-0.4
	Prof.	Work.	Diff.	Prof.	Work.	Diff.	
Cprh>cprh	13.5	11.0	2.5	12.3	11.2	1.1	-1.4
Selective>cprh	13.5	10.8	2.7	12.5	11.1	1.4	-1.3
Nosec>cprh.	11.5	10.7	0.8	12.0	11.3	0.7	-0.1

B.Upper secondary grades:

Regime change 1968-76	1954-55 cohort			1964-65 cohort			Inequal: reduced/ increased .- / +
	Men	Wom.	Diff	Men	Wom.	Diff	
Cprh>cprh.	43.8	35.1	8.7	54.0	53.3	0.7	- 8.0
Selective>cprh.	46.3	31.0	15.3	48.9	48.4	0.5	-14.8
Nosec.>cprh	37.3	21.1	16.2	44.0	53.8	-9.8	-26.0
	Dense	Disp.	Diff	Dense	Disp.	Diff	
Cprh>cprh	42.9	32.1	10.8	56.1	48.9	7.2	- 3.6
Selective>cprh.	43.8	32.6	11.2	51.9	44.3	7.6	- 2.6
Nosec>cprh	38.9	26.7	12.2	50.4	48.2	2.2	-10.0
	Prof.	*Work.*	*Diff.*	*Prof.*	*Work.*	*Diff.*	
Cprh>cprh	*70.0*	*32.1*	*37.9*	*68.1*	*43.7*	*24.4*	*-13.5*
Selective>cprh	*65.6*	*30.3*	*35.3*	*66.2*	*37.9*	*28.2*	*- 7.1*
Nosec>cprh	*40.0*	*24.9*	*15.1*	*58.8*	*41.8*	*17.0*	*+ 1.9*

In the "old" youth schools the figures that related to class trends, were diverging: class impacts increased in relation to upper secondary grades, diminished for attainment levels. These trends were strengthened by the current regime changes: the regime changes added to the increases in upper secondary grade inequalities, but were associated with some diminishing of attainment level differences.

Table 4.9. Changes in Attainment Distributions by Regime Changes from 1954-55 cohort to 1964-65cohort. Educational attainments until age 29. Output from (OLS) regression analysis.

	Attainment Levels	Upper secondary grades
Regimes & individual backgrounds	Attainment change in period	Attainment change in period
Reference case(=comprehensive regime both1968 and 1976)	10.04	10.9
Period change	-0.14	7.2
Women	0.64s	7.8s
Disp.localities	0.31s	4.0s
Parents' educ.	-0.23s	-2.6s
Prof.class	0.04	4.1
Working class	0.35s	1.3
Realskole -> comprh. school:		
Period change	-0.05	-14.0s
Women	-0.04	5.1
Disp.localities	-0.11	0.8
Parents'educ.	0.06	3.5
Prof.class	0.04	-2.2
Working class	0.35s	-3.5
No sec.school > comprh.school:		
Period change	0.50s	4.7s
Women	0.28	16.9s
Disp.localities	0.21	5.4
Parents'educ.	0.10	6.1
Prof.class	-1.10	-
Working class	0.05	-6.2

Note: s=statistically significant effect on 0.05 level

*Table 4.10 Upper Secondary Grade Impacts by Regime,
Individual Background factors, and by Interactions
between regime and Background factor. Analysis of
1954 cohort and of changes from 1954 cohort to 1962-
64 cohort. Outputs from logistic analysis (odds rates).*

Regimes,and background factors: Interactions regime * background	1954-regime effect	Impact of regime change during period
Selective68	1.11s	0.71s
No sec.school 68	0.49s	1.13
Woman	0.67s	1.32s
Dispersed locality	0.83s	1.15
Parents education	2.02s	0.90s
Professional class	1.59s	1.05
Working class	0.77s	1.03
Woman * selective regime	0.75s	1.27
Women * no.sec.sch.	0.61s	2.40s
Disp.loc.* selective regime	0.94	1.13
Disp.loc.* no sec.school	0.78	1.62
Parents'ed.* selective regime	0.95	1.19
Parents'ed.* no sec.sch.	1.00	1.33
Prof.class * realsk.regime	0.89	0.97
Prof.class * no sec.school	0.45s	1.00
Working class*selective regime	0.85	1.02
Working class*no sec.sc.	0.85	0.85
Constant		1.07

Note:The youth school condition is reference
s= Statistically significant (on 0.05) trend

When youth school regimes were introduced into municipalities that formerly had just primary schools, they produced similar distribution changes as in the former realskole-municipalities: the gender differences in attainment diminished (on both attainment indicators), but the differences reflecting parents' education and social class background grew (for class background, this effect related just to upper secondary grades, not to average attainment levels. The same changes, thus, appeared as by the former realskole municipalities).

But in addition to that, the new regime reduced the attainment differences due to *home locality*. These trends are weak in table 4.8, who shows the results from direct comparisons. They are more impressive by the regression outputs in table 4.9.

Conclusion

Studied in this chapter were the changes in attainments and attainment distributions after the introduction of comprehensive lower secondary regimes in the early 1960s and during the next ten years. A subsidiary theme related to the effect of the changes in the organization and content of the comprehensive lower secondary school after 1970. Our conclusions may be summed up this way:

1. Under the "early" "youth school" condition of the 1960s, the attainment outputs from the regimes that included a lower secondary facility within the home municipality were mostly identical. This related both to the average attainment levels, upper secondary grades and the amount of unevenness (standard deviations) of outcomes.

2. Youth from municipalities that had no secondary school within their borders were handicapped educationally, and the introduction of lower secondary schools even in these municipalities, produced significant attainment advances.

3. The "late" youth schools of the 1970s differed from their predecessors. The municipalities that had experienced early comprehensive reform, had attainment improvements in the 1970s. They also attained more evenness of outcomes. We are not able to decide what part of these improvements were due to the more "integrated"school concept, and what part was caused by the reorganization and expansion at the upper secondary stage in the 1970s. A difficulty is presented by a third factor, the shortening of the school year that was introduced in the early 1970s. It reduced the comparability of attainment levels (this issue is commented more extensively in chapter 5).

4. In the 1960s as well as around 1970, the transition to comprehensive regime brought about large diminishings of gender differences. These changes were especially large in upper secondary grades. The women

by that became the "winners" by the reform. There were similar reductions of home locality differences by the reform (especially when youth schools appeared in municipalities that formerly had no secondary school). The impacts of *class background* mostly were unaffected by the regime factor. But while the lined youth school of the 1960s was associated with smaller attainment impacts of educational background, the post-1970 transitions to comprehensive school produced *more* sensitivity to parents' education. These especially was remarkable for upper secondary grades.

In table 4.10 the redistributive trends are surveyed by help of odds ratios of upper secondary grades. Constant factor is: comprehensive regime. To the left in the table, the conditions for the 1954 cohort are shown. Below zero ratios here imply: lower attainment scores than by comprehensive organization. To the right are shown: the attainment changes that appeared by the cohorts born 1962-64: odds ratios above 1.00 here show: attainment gains above those in comprehensive municipalities.

*****

5

«UNIFICATION» AND «EXPANSION» AT THE UPPER SECONDARY STAGE

The "new" upper secondary school was a manysided reform, that inckluded new programme formats, the idea of multi-lined schools, student number increases, as well as quite new administrative and political structures. The individual counties chose different models by the implementation of the reform. Did the attainment outcomes differ?

Policies

The early 1960s debate on the future of Norwegian upper secondary education departed from the premise that the old lower secondary school, the "realskole", was doomed. However, when the Government in 1965 set up a new School Commission (the "Steen Commission") to consider the future of upper secondary education, other issues were present as well. Most youth now were expected to demand some sort of upper secondary schooling. As *vocational education* should no longer be provided at the lower secondary stage, it must be "promoted" to the upper stage.

However, the challenge from the authorities went beyond that: the new Commission also should work out a plan providing *equal opportunities* for «education and personality growth» for all 16 to 19 years olds. When the Commission in 1967 presented its design for a new upper secondary educational system, the ambitions expanded even farther.The new upper secondary school should: 1) Reflect a principle of comprehensiveness (or at least: administrative and physical unification: meaning common school-buildings, common school principals and common administrative bodies for all academic and vocational programmes at this stage. 2) Strengthen the theoretical dimension of vocational programmes, 3) Establish (at least some) combined academic-and vocational programmes, 4) Include opportunities for wandering between various programmes (- by these and other measures, the ultimate career choices should be postponed), and 5) There should be (upper) secondary education for all youth, and free choice of direction (no selection on the basis of grades). For further details see Telhaug (1975:94-109) and Lindbekk (1992:220-222).

The bringing together into one single school of many hitherto quite separate educational worlds, was assumed to produce more mutual respect and smaller cultural distance between social classes and occupational groups and by that provide more adequate preparations for an occupational life in fast change. But the commission did not (like parallel commissions in Sweden and Great Britain) stress that a redistribution of educational attainments should to take place. following the reform. The reason was maybe that a new (not-socialist)government now took office, and the reformist feared that such arguments might compromise the plan.

To attain all these objectives, there should be an administrative and physical *merger* of upper secondary academic schools («gymnas») with six other educational institutions: those for merkantile, industrial, maritime, agricultural, aestetic and household schooling, - institutions who differed in substantial contents, traditions, working methods, ways of funding, and who currently were subordinated to different Education Acts as well as different administrative authorities.

The testing-out of a new model of upper secondary education started in 1969 in two towns in the county of Nordland. In 1970 the development work spread to six other areas, including one rural municipality (Telhaug: 27-31). During this early work, the main objective was the development of programmes with equal amounts of academic and vocational stuff. In two areas it also was a question of organizing schools with an academic as well as one or more vocational programmes.

In 1974 Stortinget passed a new *Upper Secondary Education Act*, that confirmed the main ideas of the Commission. But it also responded to the strong decentralist moods of the period. The *counties* were charged with the responsibility for the development and financing of the new school system, with automatic refundment (by the Government) of about half the «normal» expense per class (the «normal expense» per class & line was to be determined by the Government). The refundings were skewed in favour of the counties who were most backward in school capacities; Here the government covered two thirds of «normal» expenses per school class, against half that in the Oslo/Akerhus area, who had the most favourable capacity situation at this stage. The individual county should itself decide on school capacities and intake numbers, choose educational programmes for the individual school, and employ staff. However, new (national) authority, the Council for Upper Secondary Education ("Råd for videregående utdanning") should was define the curricula for the various programmes and lines.

Following these changes, the Reform Agency, who prior to the reform was in firm command of reform work in primary and secondary education, now was demoted to a humbler, purely advisory role. A few years later it was abolished.

Stortinget in 1976 added a fourth equality principle to those proposed by the School Commission: that of equality between *generations*: older cohorts as well as those directly from the lower secondary stage should profit by the new opportunities: each year up to fifty percent of the vacant places in upper secondary education was be reserved for older youth, preferable youth with experience from work life (Norsk skole 1977:8). This decision produced a shortage of places that lasted even into the early 1980s. While 88-90 per cent of those who applied for intake on academic and mercantile lines, were accepted, just 67 per cent of the applicants for industrial education were admitted. Many youths who had recently graduated from the youth school, must start their upper secondary education on a different programme from their main choice (- to gather age points and other credits relevant for intake into the favoured field). At the same time pressures developed for further expansion of school capacities.

In practice, the new upper secondary concept included:

1). *Educational programmes with contents mainly inherited from particular forerunners – but adjusted so as to accomodate the reductions from six to five schooldays a week and fit into common school-day and school-year regulations (mainly descending from academic schooling). The vocational programmes were organized as discrete one-year programmes, while the customary three-year run of the academic line was retained.*

2). A *principle of multi-programme (- or multlined) school.*

3) *The individual county as main policy agents, but the decisions on the contents of the various lines was retained by the Ministry (in practice: by the new Council forUpper Secondary Education), also the patterns of cost sharing.*

4) *A large expansion of student numbers and school capacities.*

However, some practical as well as principled problems remained. To be solved by the individual county. We now shall consider them in more detail:

Lines and levels. The 1965 School Commission wanted a *theoretization* of vocational education, to reduce the cultural distance between vocational and academic programmes. This idea suffered defeat by the Government (but it was reawakened during the reform initiative of the 1990s). A more limited plan, to develop "combined" courses, with equal amounts of vocational and academic content, survived, but was just realized in a few counties (both the students and the county politicians viewed them mainly longer roads to qualifications for jobs or access to further education).

The Government settled upon a system with clearly separate «lines», at first: one academic line and five lines with vocational training (industrial, household, aestetic, maritime, and mercantile), all of them intended to provide particular job qualifications after one year, and a skilled worker certificate (or equivalent to that) after three years. The student on the academic line could choose between three mostly separate specialties (for humanist subjects, natural sciences, and social science), all of them giving access to higher education.

In a white paper, the Government in 1984 reported that the upper secondary school now had nine separate lines ("studieretninger"). In addition came some programmes for agricultural education. They were administered separatedly from the others (by the agriculture authorities). The programmes for academic issues ("allmenne fag") and industry/handicrafts ("håndverks- og industrifag") dominated the student numbers. they had 42 percent and 34.4 percent of the total intake number (Videregående opplæring, 1984:15).

The Government emphasized the importance of schooling relevant for occupational life (1984: 29, 36), and reported that the line for industry and handicrafts now had 36 separate (elementary stage) programmes for particular vocations, and 69 (advanced) programmes for these vocations (1984:23). In addition to that, the Government financed vocational training in the industry, mainly for students who had completed the elementary stage in upper secondary school. The number of intakes for such "industrial" learning was about 2000 per year (1984:33). This equalled 1-2 per cent of number who had completed a lower secondary education the same year.

The principle of *equal prestige* between lines and subject areas implied that *advanced* programmes should be developed even in the vocational subjects. This meant upgrading of the vocational subjects. These demand for upgrading were supported by school staffs as well as various local interests. In 1975, the "vocational" students made up a majority (two thirds) of the total number on elementary programmes. But the number at the next stage («advanced stage I») equalled just 34 per cent of the vocational students at the elementary stage.Those at the highest stage (advanced stage II) made up not more than 15 per cent of those on elementary programmes (parallel figures for the academic line: 94 percent and 88 percent.). While the «normal» academic student career was one of three years, that for the vocational student was commonly just a short (mostly one-year) course. These conditions changed. In 1990 the number of vocational students on advanced stage I equaled 71 per cent of the number at elementary programmes, those on advanced stage II: 39 per cent.

The five-days school-week. The introduction of a 5 days school week, in 1971-1972, created some extra challenges for the new upper secondary school: how should the accustomed levels of qualification at entry to university or to particular vocations be kept up after the instruction time per year had been cut by 14-16 percent? At the industrial lines the situation was particularly grave, the former courses in this areas had been based upon the 40 hours week of the industry. The challenges by a five-days week probably reinforced the resistance to any dilution of vocational line-contents by adding stuff from other lines or work sectors. It also made unrealistic the idea to provide occupational qualification by one single year of occupational schooling. By that it strengthened the case for advanced programmes.

Student numbers and financial strains. Expansion had been intended by those who designed the new upper secondary school, and expansion came. According to Ingebrigtsen's calculations (Ingebrigtsen 1978), the 1965 equivalents of the post 1974 upper secondary school mustered just 76.200 students. The figure was 93.200 in 1970 and 130.300 in 1977. This was not the end of the growth. In 1983 the student figure reached 167.000 (Om videregående opplæring 1984:15), in 1990 230.000 (NOS undervisnings-statistikk 1990). This equalled a tripling of the 1965-figure. The 230.000 figure should be compared with the average cohort size of the period: 60.000.

While the student numbers expanded much, the financial conditions for the teaching of the average student improved *not*. The «normal» expenses per class that at an early stage were laid down by the Government, to serve as a basis for the Government's financial support, were not revised. The main reason for this «freezing» of the expenses considered needed, was probably the fast growth of student numbers (which contrasted sharply with the stable condition at the compulsory stage). For county budgets, the impacts of these student numbers were severe, and improvement beyond the Government's norm was out of question. In «academic» programmes, the «normal» expense of the Government provided for 37½ instructor «periods» per week per class (Telhaug 1975:91-93, Norsk skole 1976:4). This figure should be compared with the 47½ hour, considered «normal» for a school class at (a large) lower secondary school. The formula for the «academic» upper secondary education in practice, assumed a continuation of the one hour-one class-room-one teacher principle of the old academic upper secondary school.

On the basis of data on expenses per student in compulsory school and at academic lines in secondary education 1975 to 1992 (Sørensen 1995:table 2, and Falk/Rattsø 1995:table1), it may be calculated that the relations between the expenses per student in upper secondary education and in compulsory education changed radically during the period, from 1.60 in 1975 (reflecting the higher wages and lower teaching loads of upper secondary school teachers) to 0.99. The «normal» expenses for industry- and household classes were set higher (154 and 172 per cent of those for «academic» classes. See Norsk skole 1976:4), to take care of equipment, working materials - and that the classes for security reasons should be smaller in these subjects. Despite this, the figures confirm the negative development for upper secondary programmes, and that the conditions allowed little development work or extra services for particular catergories of upper secondary students.

Schools. The physical building-out patterns after 1975 may have aggravated these conditions. Following demands for decentralism, many of the new schools were small, even if they were intended to house more than one single line. The In school year 1980-1981, Norway had altogether 962 upper secondary schools. 498 had less than one hundred students (NOS: Educational statistics 1980: table 22). But the Government's financiation formula contained no extra means for small schools, comparable to those in compulsory education. Ingebrigtsen's analysis of 1977 budgets (Ingebrigtsen1982) makes it clear that the counties did not award extra money from their own budgets to compensate for the particular conditions at small schools.

The counties as policy agents.

The «new» upper secondary school met a number of external factors: 1. A new authority structure, that gave reign to new interests, 2. Demands for equality between subject areas. 3. Some unforeseen bottlenecks. 4..Qualification demands that in some cases were at odds with the confines by a shortened school week, 5 Cost sharing patterns, that differed between the individual counties, and that"froze" the amounts of instruction of the various programmes, commonly at a lower level than was expected during the preparation of the reform.

The working out of solutions to the problems that emerged, was left to each individual county. The decisions related to total capacities and their distributions between lines, the locations and dimensionings of new schools, what lines the indivual school should have, and how the various schools should they should be organized, particularly if they should have just one line, or two, three or more.

As a consequence, the new upper secondary school reform was not implementad as one uniform reform, but in versions that differed between the counties, depending upon the the «mix» of policies of the individual county.

Table 5.1 Student numbers in Upper Secondary Education 1976-1981 By county.

COUNTY	Students per 100 17-19 years 1976	Students per 100 rank 1976	Student number increase 1976-1981 (percent)	Stud.ent Number increase. 1976-81. rank
Oslo/Akershus	78.1	1	0.5	18
Aust-Agder	68.6	2	7.1	17
Vest-Agder	69.2	3	17.5	12
Nord-Trøndelag	67.7	4	24.2.	6
Sør-Trøndelag	67.5	5	13.9	15
Oppland	63.1	6	19.4	10
Hedmark	62.7	7	13.1	16
Hordaland	62.2	8	17.9	11
Buskerud	61.8	9	16.6	13
Rogaland	61.3	10	16.1	14
Vestfold	59.8	11	30.5	4
Sogn/Fjordane	58.7	12	20.3	9
Østfold	58.5	13	20.6	8
Troms	56.7	14	35.2	3
Møre/Romsdal	56.5	15	22.4	7
Telemark	54.1	16	25.4	5
Nordland	52.5	17	36.7	2
Finmark	43.5	18	55.2	1

Table 5.1 ranks the counties by upper secondary student numbers per 17 to 19 years old in 1976. These figures reflect the capacities just before the new Act was adopted. The Oslo/Akershus figure (78.1) implies that the student number here equaled three fourths of the relevant birth cohorts.

The Finmark figure (bottom of the table) was half that in Oslo/Akershus. The distribution of student numbers between the counties in 1976 reflected the policies and developments just before the 1974 Act. Notable is that the rank order correlation between the 1976 distributions and the same counties' expansion rates 1970 to 1975 was 0.75. However, when, after 1974, the individual counties became the main actors in upper secondary policies, quite new trends appeared. In the Oslo/Akershus region, there was a complete standstill in upper secondary student numbers from 1976 to 1981. Finmark increased its student number (per 17-19 years old) by more than fifty percent. The policy changes are reflected in the rank order shown to the right in the table. The rank order correlation between the 1976 figures and the 1976-81 increases is minus 0.76. The new regime, thus, produced an expansion that compensated for the former differences in upper secondary capacity (as well as a radical - one might even say: abrupt - change in relation to the building out policies prior to the new upper secondary education act.

The counties also differed in the *«balances»* that developed between *academic and vocational programmes.* Around 1975, the distributions of students between academic and vocational subjects were similar (52-55 percent on academic issues) in the various parts of the country (except that the academic line had a smaller proportion of the upper secondary student numbers in the Northern counties). After 1975 a clear difference appeared between the Oslo/Akershus region and other areas. In 1981, 51.7 per cent of the new students in Oslo were admitted into the academic line. The figure for Akershus county was 41.6 per cent. The proportion on academic subjects was 33 percent in the rest of the country (NOS, Educational Statistics, October 1981: 84). In Finmark the figure was just 26.1. During the same year, the academic upper secondary grades made up 50.1 percent of total number of programme completions in Oslo/Akershus area (a complete academic upper secondary grade («gymnaseksamen») here is set equal to three one-year programme completions), against 38 per cent in the rest of the country. The Oslo/Akershus area participated just to a minor extent in the expansion of vocational education i the period.

In 1969, when the first versions new model were tried out, the upper secondary sector consisted of just *one-line* schools. During the developments 1970 to 1983, some counties were consistently ahead of the others in faithfulness to the multi-line principle (See table 5.2). In 1977, the average numbers of lines per school were 2.6, 1.7, and 1.7 in the counties of Hedmark, Telemark, and Møre. In 1983 the figures were 2.5 to 1.9. Now less than one third of the academic lines in these counties were at schools with just one single line. In contrast to that, Buskerud, Vestagder and Hordaland had 1.1-1.3 lines per school in 1977, 1.3 to 1,6 in 1983, and around 80 per cent of their academic lines were even now at schools with just that line. These two groups of counties thus present quite different profiles in school development Below, they are termed "progressive" and "conservative". Both areas had moderate student number growths during the

Table 5.2. County Policies in the Multi-line Issue, 1973 1977,1983.

	1973	1977	1983
Number of «lines» per school (average)			
1.0-1.49	10	6	2
1.5-1.99	0	4	7
2.o or more	0	9	10
Academic «lines» at one-line schools:			
Two thirds or more	19	5	3
Between one third and two thirds	0	12	9
One third or less	0	2	7

period: 20 and 17 percent, and larger proportions of their new students in 1981 related to vocational lines.

*****

Common for the nineteen reforming counties were: : Administrative integration of the political/administrative activities relating to upper secondary schooling, plus unification of the formats the lines and programmes at this stage, also relating to the number of school weeks and instruction period per week.But the counties differed in their amounts of expansion, subject emphasis, and committment to the multi-line principle. When the various choices of each county are observed, four different reform regimes emerge:

1.The Oslo/Akershus area: Here no expansion appeared. The former emphasis on academic subject areas was maintained. But at some schools multi-line organization was introduced. (In 1983, the average number of lines per school was 1.9). .

2.The expansion area in the North, which in the main related to vocational subjects. Here no consistent policy in the multi-line school. issue appeared

3. Progressive (multi-line) school organization. Moderate expansion of capacities, with an emphasis on vocational subjects.

4. Conservative (one-line) school organization maintained. Moderate expansion of capacities, with an emphasis on vocational subjects..

The regimes of ten of the nineteen counties are covered by this typology.

Attainment impacts of upper secondary regimes. Total attainments.

Table 5.3 shows how the attainments changed from the 1954 cohort to that born ten years later. We note an average attainment level increase that amounts to 0.2 years, and the number of upper secondary (third year) graduates increased by about one third.

However, these changes can not just be attributed to the upper secondary education reform; they also reflect the changes at the lower secondary stage and in higher education in this period. More light is thrown upon the effects of the upper secondary reform by the other figures in table 5.3, where a number of differences between regimes appear.

The Oslo/Akershus figures relate to the most limited version of the reform. In this particular area, the authorities one were loyal to the multi-line principle, but the capacities and subject emphasis changed little or not at all. In this area followed a small *decline* in average attainment levels, but the number of graduates continued growing. The data indicate that there was some reallocation of resources - in favour of full three-year grade completions, at the expense of other programmes.

The expansive North area had a different development: we observe larger attainment levels increases than by the other regimes, but smaller increase in upper secondary grade completions, smaller even than in not-expanding Oslo/Akershus. We conclude that the new resources the were set in in here mainly furthered elementary programme activities.

The two lines presented at the bottom of the table show some impacts of the contrasting principles of school organization. The »progressive» counties gained more than those who kept to older ways. This trend contradicts the Trøndelag-findings of Bonesrønning (1996), who compared individual schools within this particular county, with focus on grade scores.

.   .

To look more into the effect of organization patterns, these we studied the post-reform patterns of mobility between upper secondary lines («studieretninger»). Did the regime differences produce different career patterns? Between 1986 and 1987, 17.2 per cent of the upper secondary students (that is: of those who remained in upper secondary education) changed line («studieretning»). Did the number of mobiles differ between the counties? Our data show that 21.5 per cent of the students in counties with progressive regime changed line between these years, against 15 per cent of the students in conservative counties. The difference (statistically significant) confirms the inter-line mobility effect by multi-programme schools. But the students who changed lines, had fewer (third year) grade completions than those who kept to their original line, and the "mobiles" with an upper secondary grade, proceeded seldom to higher education. In sum, the "openness" of these schools, was mostly a neutral factor for final attainments.

Table 5.3. Attainment changes from 1954 cohort to 1964 cohort. By County Policy.

Policy	Attainm.levels:		Upper Sec.grades		Sample sizes:	
	1954 cohort	Change during period	1954 cohort	Change during period	1954	1964
Country as whole	11.45	0.21	38.0	13.6	5084	5233
Oslo/Akershus	11.89	-0.11	45.5	9.6	785	893
Expansive North	11.15	0.36	32.7	8.1	443	464
Progressive	11.36	0.28	37.5	12.2	631	746
Conservative	11.54	0.24	41.8	11.5	850	959

The financial regime of the new upper secondary school was intended to reduce the educational differences between the various counties.. Prior to the reform (= for the 1954 cohort), the attainment averages of *individual counties* on average deviated 0.20 from the *national* average. Within the 1964 cohort, the inter-county deviance was exactly the same. In upper secondary grades, the inter-county deviance increased from 3.5 percent to 5.2 percent. It therefore is evident that the intention to diminish the attainment differences between counties, was not fulfilled.

Attainment impacts of upper secondary regimes. The impacts of background conditions.

Robert Erikson (1996: 38-39) found no class equalization following the postwar expansions in the Swedish educational system. He proposed that this partly was because the mobilization of women (large, especially during the later part of this expansion) mainly came in the higher social strata. He also argued that the various classes differed less in general school-motivation than in the *contents* of their school interests (1996:26, 32). Because of that, the various attempts to bring the school world closer to common people had small effect, as long as the substantive content of the schooling did mot match their career interests better.

Implication for our own case: The content of the various educational programmes counts more for class differences in attainments than other other regime factors do. In our case: the status for vocational subjects within the «new» upper secondary school might appeal to working class youth, at the same time as the working class number with «academic» choices goes down. Another outcome: Because of the lasting«academic emphasis» in Oslo/Akershus, there will be no working class mobilization in this area.

Other policy outcomes: geographical decentralism furthered recruitment from "milieus" where secondary schooling previously was uncommon. But the limited teaching resources, especially in peripheral areas, hindered the development of adequate pedagogical services these places. Multi-line school patterns may have attracted youth with unclear preferences, who were inclined to postpone ultimate career choices. This may have furthered the recruitment of women and working class youth .

Table 5.3A. Post-reform Attainment Levels (at Age 27-28), by Upper Secondary Regime. 1964-65 cohort.

	ALL	OSLO/ AKERSHUS	EXPANSIVE NORTH	PROGRES- SIVE REGIME	CONSER- VATIVE REGIME
Men	11.60	11.65	11.69	11.57	11.60
Women	11.67	11.95	11.38	11.69	11.68
Densely pop.area	11.79	11.68	11.70	11.80	11.80
Dispersed Population	11.43	11.41	11.00	11.30	11.42
Ed.backgr. Effect*	1.47	1.16	1.36	2.01	1.64
Profess. backgr.	12.20	12.31	11.90	12.60	12.80
Working class	11.30	10.80	10.92	10.70	11.00

*Attainment differences between parents with education score 6-4 and parents with education score 1-0.

Shown in table 5.3 is how the post-reform attainment differences by gender, home location, class and educational background varied between regimes. The table relates to the 1964-65 cohort (that is: a cohort, whose upper secondary entries mainly came in 1981-1983).

We first compare the patterns of distribution in Oslo/Akershus and in the North counties. These regimes differed in *expansiveness* as well as *academic/vocational balance.*

Here a dramatic difference appear in relation to the gender scores In Oslo/Akershus a clear female superiority appears; in attainment level average as well as in upper secondary grades. In the Northern area, the opposite condition holds. Observed is further that the men's attainments cores are mostly identical in the two areas, and the men's figures are close to those for the nation as a whole. While those for the women fluctuate wildly; in Oslo/Akershus, they are much higher than nationally, in the Northern area they are much below.

Notable is also: In the North, the attainment differences between densely populated areas and more peripheral areas double those in Oslo/Akershus (both places the attainment figures for the dense areas are close to those for the country as a whole, while those for the periphery are much below that), the impacts of educational background differ (much greater impact in the North, especially in relation to upper secondary grades). The class impacts on attainment also differ, but they were *smaller* in the North. In Oslo/Akershus, the «professionals'» attainments are slightly above the national figures, but those for working class youth are much *smaller* than for the country as a whole. But in the North, both the working class figures and those relating to professional background were below, those for professional background especially much below. In short: the educational impacts of class difference became smaller in the North, while those of gender, location and educational background became larger. The Oslo/Akershus regime did not further class equalization in educational attainment, but it mobilized the women very effectively. It also seems to have limited the impact of educational background.

The figures are in line with the observations by Robert Erikson, with reference to the school development in Sweden, (more theoretically inclined and less expanding then the Norwegian, and by that: more similar to that of Oslo/Akershus): it furthered the mobilization of women, but appealed little to youth from working class backgrounds.

Relating to the impacts of *school organization*, notable differences between regimes appear for the educational background impacts (they are larger by multi-line organization). The attainment scores for youth from professional background is similar by the two regimes, those for working

Table 5.3B. Post-reform Completion of Upper Secondary Grades. By Regime and Individual Background. 1964-65 cohort.

	ALL	OSLO/ AKERSHUS	EXPANSIVE NORTH	PROGRES- SIVE	CONSER- VATIVE
Men	52.9	52.0	53.2	51.3	48.0
Women	52.6	60.6	43.3	53.9	56.5
Densely pop.area	55.2	52.8	53.4	57.0	55.7
Dispersed Population	47.1	48.0	32.2	48.0	48.1
Ed.backgr. Effect*	25.7	24.0	34.8	40.0	33.5
Profess. Backgr.	64.2	67.3	57.8	69.7	69.6
Working class	43.3	35.2	35.2	30.7	39.6

*Attainment differences between parents with education score 6-4 and parents with education score 1-0.

class background is lower by multi-line school organization.

Our material show larger between-lines mobility in multi-line counties than in the counties where most seecondary schools had just one single line. By multi-line conditions, 21.5 percent of the students (who remained in upper secondary schooling 1986 to 1987) changed line, against 15 percent of the students in single-line areas. This difference (statistically significant) confirms that «progressive»organization made for more mobility between lines. But youth from working-class backgrounds or whose parents had small «educational capital», profited little by this.

Here, we have neither corrected for interactions between background factors nor for pre-reform conditions. An (OLS) regression analysis of the cohorts born 1954-55 and 1964-65, that entered background factors as well as pre-reform attainment distributions was carried out. Within the Oslo/Akershus area the women and the youth from dispersed population areas had statistically significant attainment increases from the 1954-55 cohort to the 1964-65 cohort. A deterioration of working class attainments appeared in this area, but this trend was not statistically significant. In «progressive» counties (compared with the «conservative» counties), the attainments of women and the educational background impacts (on attainment levels as well as grades) increased during the period studied, but these changes were too small to attain statistical significance.

In the North, the attainment differences between home locality types were large even before the reform. But, the sample's number of persons from this area was small, and gave not a good basis for firm conlusions on the impacts of the new regime.

Conclusion

1. The upper secondary reform of the 1970s was a more complex reform

than that on the lower secondary stage: it involved a quite new set of authorities and mechanisms for the channeling resources, and made for heterogeneous developments between counties.

2. The reform brought about large but very uneven growths in the student numbers at the upper secondary stage, and considerable redistribution of educational capacities between counties. However, the correlation between attainment level developments and upper secondary grades became loose. and the general attainment differences between the counties did not diminish,

3. The post-reform regimes differed in their expansion rates, faithfulness

to the principle of multi-line schools, and balances between vocational and academic lines. They had different attainment impacts. Particularly

notable were the mobilizations of women in multi-line counties and in not-expanding, "gymnas-marked Oslo/Akershus. But these two regimes diverged in their impacts on class background effects.

4. The data support the Erikson observation of an inverse relation between educational mobilizations of women and of the working class

In chapters 6 and 7 we shall return to these trends, in the light of data that even include the changes in higher education and in compulsory school.

******

6

ATTAINMENT INCREASES BY THE REFORMS?

The attainments grew during the period we have observed.
Which reforms caused that growth?

Period of growth.

Between 1957 and 1975, the percentage of the Norwegian GNP devoted to educational purposes increased from 4.0 to 6.7. The number of pupils in compulsory school stabilized, but after 1960 came a tripling of the numbers in upper secondary and higher education. In the course of the years separate the cohorts born in 1954-55 and 1964-65, the average levels of attainment went up from 11.06 to 11.61. The attainment deviation shrank radically, from 2.30 to 1.76. Surprisingly, there was almost no change in the percentage that completed a higher education programme. The percentage went from 21.7 to 22.4 (criterion: completion of the elementary year of a professional or semi-professional programme, or completion of the universities' general preparatory programme (examen philosophicum). In other words: the number with secondary education increased, but little of that expansion was carried over into higher education.

These figures relate to attainments until age 27 (28 for those born in 1954 or 1964). However, the schooling went on even after that age. In 1992, when the 1954-55 cohort was 37 (or 38), its attainment average reached 11.49. Now, 26.5 percent completed some programme in higher education. The university expansion after 1990 provided a second chance for the younger cohort. Its higher education number now certainly advanced beyond the 22.4 percent that was observed in 1992.

Two cohorts - two sets of regimes.

Was the attainment advance of the younger cohort produced by the *reforms* that this cohort experienced, or the general changes in social welfare, abilities and motivation during these years?

The *1954-55 cohort* profited by the "new deal" in rural areas, that especially furthered school quality in peripheral communities. Most municipalities had implemented the (early version of) the new lower secondary school, the other municipalities were still served by the "old" regime: a selective, lower secondary school ("realskole"), in many cases one that was not even situated within one's own municipality. At the upper secondary stage was a number of specialized school ("academic" schools or schools for particular occupations). Designs for a new, "decentralizing", policy had been presented for higher education, promising new facilities in the geographical regions that had no university. The main outcome so far was a Stortinget decision to establish new universities in Tromsø and Trondheim. But the full effect of the new higher education policy lay in the future.

The *later* cohort was served by lower secondary schools, that by now was fully established in all municipalities (in the form of "comprehensive", "integrated" schools), commonly there were even such schools in all the villages of that municipality. A completely new school pattern had been established at the upper secondary stage, expanded, "decentralized, often in the form of "multi-lined" schools. The district" plan for higher education had produced "district colleges", post-secondary schools, with a wide spectre of programmes.

Regime differences in attainment.

Table 6.1 shows how the attainments of the 1964-65 cohort varied by regime (rather: by the type of *regime change* that the individual person

Table 6.1. Attainments by Regime Development 1968-1980.
1964-65 Cohort at Age 27 (28).

REGIMES	Attainm. level Average	Attainm level. SD.	Higher educ. compl.	N
Decentr.primary pattern maintained	11.48	2.00	18.6	233
Selective, after that :cprh. lower secondary reg.	11.41	2.13	21.0	1568
No secondary, after that: cprh.lower secondary	11.44	1.95	19.1	424
Cphr.lower sec. maintained	11.45	2.11	21.5	8504
"Old"upper sec., after that: not-expansive "new"	11.56	2.17	26.0	1823
"Old"upper sec., after that: expansive "new" regime	11.18	1.95	15.1	925
"Old"upper sec,. after that: "progressive" "new reg.	11.48	2.05	15.1	1450
"Old" upper sec.,after that: "conservative" new reg.	11.62	2.11	23.6	1889
"District" policy area	11.43	2.10	20.4	6751
University area	11.52	2.11	23.2	3745

had experienced 1968 to 1976). A main observation is that the upper secondary policies were the more critical factors: the highest attainments appeared by the "conservative" or "not-expanding" regimes, the lowest came in the expansive counties in the North.

Table 6.2 shows changes *between* the two cohorts. A regression analysis eliminates the impacts of the regimes experienced at other stages of the individual career. At the bottom of the table (line 9) is shown a constant factor the was calcultaled for this combination of conditions: 1."Normal primary school pattern, 2) Comprehensive school even for the 1954-55 cohort ("youth school" within the home municipality), 3) Average upper secondary conditions in the 1970s (=average amounts of expansion and of multi-linearity), 4) University county. This combination of conditions approximates a "reform-free" condition, where the attainment change just reflect the impact of "period factors" external to the educational system. Under these conditions the attainment changes were small: a small increase in average attainment levels, a small decrease in higher education completions. The column to the right, shows the output by a logistic regression of the higher education completions, which supports that it declined. One might argue that the Oslo/Akershus condition implies even more of regime stability, at the school capacity was at a stand-still. For this condition a yero-growth appeared in average attainment levels, and a more pronounced decline in higher education completions.

The table shows altogether seven significant divergent trends from that by the conbination of reference factors at the bottom of the table. Two of these diverging trends (line 3) relate to attainment changes after secondary comprehensive schools appeared in municipalities who formerly had no secondary facilities. Even the regression coefficient (B-score) for higher education indicates large increase, but because of small numbers, the deviation is not statistically significant. But the odds ratio 1.66 is.

Line 4 shows significant declines in attainments under the Oslo-Akershus by change in administrative and general "formats" for upper secondary programmes, but no expansion of school capacity. The "districts" (line 8) gained in attaient levels as well as higher education completions (only the first of these gains were statistically significant). The conservative counties (line 7) gained (significantly for attainment levels), while the Northern counties (line 5) harvested negative attainment developments (significant for higher education completions).

Of great principal interest are the attainment developments that accompanied the transition from a selective to a comprehensive lower secondary regime. Some figures in Chapter 4 indicated attainment setbacks after this regime change. The Table 6.2 figures correct this conclusion. Line 2 shows almost identical attainment developments by the two regimes.

Also notable is that the municipalities with decentralized primary school organization now slipped behind the "normal" counties in attainments (line 1). The attainment changes were similar to those in the Oslo/-Akershus area. If Oslo/Akershus regime is considered to represent the no-change condition, the "decentralist" primary school regimes just joined this area in its downward attainment development.

Table 6.2. Attainment Changes from 1954-55 Cohort to
1964-65 Cohort. Impacts of Regime Developments 1968-1980.
Linear and logistic regression coefficients..

Regime change	Attainm.level change reg.coeff.	Higher educ. change reg.coeff.	Higher educ, change odds.ratio
1.Decentr.prim.school sch. pattern maintained.	-0.30	-8.1	0.69
2,Selective low.sec->cprh regime	0.07	-0.2	0.99
3.No secondary school ->cprh.regime	0.54s	8.1	1.66s
4.Old upper sec-regime >not-expanding,"new" upper secondary regime	-0.26s	-9.8s	0.64
5.Old upper sec.regime ->expansive,"new" upper secondary regime	-0.20	-3.6s	0.76
6.Old upper sec-regime -> progressive,"new" upper sec. regime	0.08	0.4	1.02
7.Old upper sec. regime ->conservative,"new" upper sec.ondary regime	0.18s	0.3	1.02
8."District"policy area	0.49s	1.4	1.09
9.Constant	0.22	-1.6	0.90

s=statistically significant effect on .95% level

Our analysis in chapter 5 observed a diminishing of attainment levels in Oslo/Akershus, while this area advanced in upper secondary grades. Table 6.2 gives a more consistent picture: showing significant attainment decreases (in relation to the reference factor) on both measures. More detailed analyses of attainments confirm that the number with upper secondary grades went up, but this gain was not carried over into higher education.

A main observation from table 6.2 is that some of the reform impacts that appeared when the analysis was limited to one particular stage, now evened out. This particularly related to the outcome by change from a selective lower secondary regime to a comprehensive regime. Table 6.2 shows that the two regimes were equally effective from the point of view of educational mobilization. It remains to be seen if the two regimes even were neutral for individual background factors impacts. We shall return to that in chapter 7.

However, *some* other regime effects emerge *clearer* in table 6.2 than in previous analyses: This above all related to the attainment gains in the municipalities that formerly had no secondary facilities, and those that accompanied the higher education developments in "districts".

Implications of shorter school year.

For the school year 1972-73 (and the period that followed) Stortinget introduced a «planning week», that reduced the number of school weeks from 38 to 37 per year. This change related to both the stages in secondary school. From the school year 1973-74, this reduction of the number of school weeks was joined by a reduction of the number of instruction periods per week in lower secondary school from 36 to 30, due to the introduction of a 5-days school week. The next year a similar the reduction came at the upper secondary stage. The municipalities were allowed to introduce the same reduction for the primary school.

These reductions of school hours came in the course of the period that separates the school careers of the cohorts born 1954-55 and 1964-65. - What was the impact of these changes for the total amount of schooling of these cohorts?

These effects appeared after our two cohorts had completed their primary stage schooling. But they "hit" the secondary stage schooling of the two cohorts differently. In table 6.3 we present the secondary education impacts for the various birth cohorts .

Following these changes, the number of instruction periods per school year decreased from 1368 to 1110, that is by 19 percent. The reduction for an entire (six year) "secondary" programme was exactly that: 19 per cent. Between the 1954-55 cohort and the 1964-65 cohort, the diminishing of instruction time (for a complete 6 year programme) made up 17 percent. In the course of six school years this adds up to 1.02 school years. Because not all members of the 1954-65 cohort completed the upper secondary grade, their average number of upper secondary school years should rather be set to two, and the "reduction factor" adds up to 0.85. Implication: the average school level attained by the 1964-65 cohort (11.61) should be reduced by an amount of 0.85 to be comparable to that of the earlier cohort. In that case, the attainment gain during the period shrinks to zero.

This conclusion equals that arrived at by Riksaasen (1983), who found that the nineth year of compulsory schooling just compensated for the loss of school time during all the preceding years.

Table 6.3.Number of instruction periods in secondary school. 1953 cohort to 1965 cohort

Birth cohort	Number of years x instr. periods	Sum instr. periods	Average for whole programme	Sum instruction as percentage of 1953
1953	6 x 1368	8208	8208	100
1954	5 x 1368 1 x 1332	8172	8043	98
1955	4 x 1368 1 x 1332 1 x 1110	7914	8043	98
1964	6 x 1110	6660	6669	81
1965	6 x 1110	6660	6660	81

Whether these reductions were distributed evenly between the school years, or came at the end (in form of earlier school-leaving), the impacts on the amount of knowledge and learning ought to be the same. A person who completed the upper secondary grade, then would have completed one year less of secondary schooling when entering higher education. And the entire cohort's *formal* advance in average attainment (0.61years for the cohort as a whole) did not fully compensate for the reduction in school "intensity".

This may explain the leveling off in higher education attainments. Maybe, the content, methods and scholastic demands in higher education had not been tuned to the changes in curricula and ambitions at lower stages. And fewer of the graduates from upper secondary school were, following that, prepared for the demands they met at the university.

*****

Conclusion.

1. Observed were clear changes (increases) in "formal" attainments. These changest were mainly due to the new "district policies" in higher education and the "decentralization" of lower secondary facilities, associated with the establishing of lower secondary schools in all municipalities, But the increases in upper secondary capacities were not associated with similar advances: Attainment decreases appeared in the counties with no increase in total capacity as well as by very large capacity increases. While the counties with moderate expansion had some (small) attainment increases.

2. The secondary school issues (selective/comprehensive school, single-line/multiple-line school), that coloured the reform debate in this period, were of minor importance for the attainment outcomes.

*****

7

EQUALIZATION AND ITS CAUSES

Four levels of educational reform are treated in a unified analysis. Had the new regimes any effect as redistributors of educational attainment?

A trend that vanished?

In the course of this century, the Western countries restructured their primary school systems; from the 1980s most youth got some measure of secondary education, and universities lost its traditional elite status. Further education was accessible for all, and (mostly) free of pay.

But, recent studies have thrown doubt upon the results of these endeavours. Was a "broader" educational participation in fact attained? A main conclusion from the ambitious 13 nation study, a comparative analysis of some modern, industrial countries, was that no reduction in class-based selection came about during recent years, even though some figures on developments in Sweden and the Netherlands presented more complex trends (Blossfeld and Shavitt 1993). If any equalization occurred after 1980, it just related to particular sub-categories among the youth (Erikson and Jonsson 1993, de Graaf and Ganzeboom 1993).

This conclusion may be explained in various ways: one might argue that even if variations in geographical locality and family economy now have small explanatory value for school participation, school success still is conditional upon a number of non-economical factors who are distributed skewly (and correlated with social class): particular value orientations, network positions, and individual or collective personality factors.

In their study of recent developments in Swedish education, Erikson and Jonsson disclaimed the analytical relevance of class-related differences in family economy and values (1996:26 and 105): The various strata now neither differ in principled attitudes to schooling nor in their commands of the skill, knowledges or personality traits that are basic to school work; but in the 1980s, the various classes had different views on what educations were worth their while (p.32). Some people also believe that the person's amount of education counts less for incomes than previously (p.131). Grøgaard's recent (1993) Oslo-material seems to support this assumption.

These views are contrary to the well-established theories by Blau and Duncan (1967) and others, that industrial societies to an increasing extent are achievement- and qualification-oriented (- and by implication: that careers increasingly became school-dependent). But recent evidence from Irish research shows that even the early phase of industrialization was not associated with more qualification-geared employment practices than previously (Breen and Whelan 1944). Even in the 1980s, particularism had large impacts on appointments and promotions (Hout 1989:319-312).

Maybe the new developments in educational recruitment were due to equalization of wages and living conditions in the later part of the 20th century, which opened new opportunities for able youth, additional to those by ever more education.

Norway did not participate in the 13nation study. But two studies of higher education recruitment around 1990 supported that a freezing of recruitment patterns occurred even here, at least in higher education (Knudsen et al.1993, Nordli Hansen 1995). The Grøgaard study showed a pronounced trend among upper secondary students from skilled worker-backgrounds to prefer technical training to academic studies in engineering even, if they were well qualified for entry to (academic) engineering school. The implication seems to be: When the distributions of incomes and opportunities become more «equal», more youth will make choices in line with their parents'. Such choices may be supported by particular value preferences and considerations of network: educational and occupational choices that imply continuations of background, give advantages that one had to forsake by other lines of advance.

In this chapter we shall inquire more closely if the equalization of educational attainments continued in the late postwar period, particularly during the 1980s. We also want to see if the changes in pattern of distributions that occurred (if any) were due to particular educational reforms, or if they were caused by more general social processes. - While recruitment trends that were due to particular reforms, may be expected to vanish after the first post reform-cohorts have passed through the system, those who represent more general processes (external to the education system) will have more lasting effects.

Table 7.1. Educational attainments at Age 27 (28) by Gender, Home Locality, Parents' Education and Class. Cohorts born 1954-55 and 1964-65.

	Attainment levels 1954-55 1964-65		Higher education 1954-55 1964-65	
Total sample	11.0	11.9	21.7	22.3
SD	2.3	2.08		
Gender:				
Men	11.4	11.8	22.3	19.8
Women	10.8	11.9	21.3	25.6
Home locality				
Densely populated	11.3	11.9	25.8	26.4
Dispersed population	10.7	11.6	16.3	18.6
Parents' education (sum)				
1 (lowest)	10.6	11.4	17.8	15.0
6 (highest)	13.7	14.1	68.1	64.8
Parents' class:				
Professional	12.2	12.7	43.1	39.4
Intermediate	10.9	11.7	21.0	20.3
Manual work	10.4	11.2	13.5	13.0
"No class"	9.9	11.2	13.1	13.7

Equalization even after 1970?

In table 7.1, the cohorts born 1954-55 and 1964-65 are compared for educational attainments until age 27 or 28. In 1982, when the earlier of these cohorts was 27 (alternatively: 28 years), the average attainment level was 11. 22 per cent had completed a higher education programme. At the same age, the 1964-65 cohort had an average attainment level amounting to 11.5. Their percentage with higher education completions now had risen to 22 percent.

Relating to the 1954-55 cohort: Table 7.1 shows some clear attainment differences by individual backgrounds at age 27-28. In 1982 the average gender difference in higher education was 1 per cent (in favour of the men); The difference between home localities was as large as 9.5. While 43 per cent of the youth from professional background had some amount of higher education, the figure for working class youth was below one third of that. The differences by educational background were even larger: those from the lowest stage had only one sixth as large higher education representation as those from the top stage.

Table 7.1 shows that the attainment differences due to gender and locality decreased in the course of the period that separates the cohorts; The women now came clearly ahead of the men in the number with higher education, but in attainment levels the figures were about the same for the two genders. There also was a decrease in the differences associated with class background.

Table 7.2 presents the same material by means of OLS- and logistic regressions (odds rates). The coefficients reported in the lower part of the table are the ones most pertinent to our questions.

The attainment level data (left hand column) show that the men lost their attainment superiority, the impacts of home locality and of the parents' education diminished, also that between professional and "intermediate" classes and working class (= reference category for these). The reduction in men's "supremacy" is especially impressive: male superiority was reduced by about 0.6 years in education level, and by 6.8 in higher education rates.

Some of these reductions of differences are statistically significant (marked by «s» in the table): those of gender (both indicators), and those of other classes or working class (reference category for these classes). The odds rates for higher education impacts (extreme right column) show general impact decreases (= odds rates below 1.00) for all the factors analyzed. But only that for gender ("men", with women as reference) was significant. The odds rates for the other factors are so close to 1.00 that the safest conclusion is that no impact change occurred.

In sum: the figures in table 7.2 support that the equalization of educational attainments continued through the 1980s; but the changes were uneven. The advances of the women are quite convincing, to some extent even the recession for youth from professional backgrounds. But the changes in impacts of localities, educational background and intermediate class background were less clear and limited to average attainment levels.

We argued that the educational mobilization of women interacted with the other background factors. Erikson and Jonsson found (1996:38-39) that the

Table 7.2 Changes in attainment effects of Background Factors from 1954-55 cohort to 1964-65 cohort. (OLS) Regression Coefficients and Odds ratios.

	Attainment, (OLS) reg. Coefficient	Higher education. (OLS)reg. coefficient.	Higher education Odds ratio
1954-55 cohort:			
Men	0.41 s	0.6	1.04
Densely pop.area	0.10 s	-0.5	1.19
Parents' educ.	0.55 s	9.3 s	1.38 s
Prof.class	0.80 s	11.5 s	2.01 s
Interm.class	0.46 s	5.6 s	1.62 s
"No class"	-0.44 s	0.1	0.99
Changes during period:			
General trend	1.29 s	4.6 s	1.32 s
Men	-0.59 s	-8.2 s	0.60 S
Densely pop. area	-0.10	-0.5	0.94
Parents' educ.	-0.10 s	-0.9	0.99
Prof.class	-0.17	-1.1 s	0.99
Interm.class	-0.08 s	-0.3	0.97
"No class"	0.37 s	-1.2	0.95
Constant	9.49	2.0	

s=statistically significant effect on 0.05 level.

growth of female (educational) participation in Sweden during the late 80s was associated with a more class-based recruitment, that out-weighed an (opposite) class-trend in men's careers. Norwegian data (Lindbekk 1998:157) confirmed this. Also appearing among the Norwegian men were reductions in the impacts of educational background and professional class (statistically significant on four of the six OLS-regression indicators that were studied. The same trend but not statistically significant differences appeared by odds rates). However, among the women, the impacts of class difference *increased* (statistically, no significant change). And for them no changes in the impacts of educational background appeared.

Our conclusion therefore is: the *class impact* trend demonstrated for several trend weakened after 1980, and now it related just to the men. The impact of *educational* background was greater and more stable than that of class background. But it was not quite stable. Among men, the attainment impact of parents' education clearly diminished, and even among women some (very weak) impact reductions appeared.

But the diverging trend for the two genders - visible both in relation to class and educational background effects - indicates a more unstable situation for these recruitment factors. The vast changes in educational policies around 1990 may have contributed to this. But firm conclusions demand data on more recent cohorts than those surveyed in the chapters above.

Data relating to men and women born *1969-70*, (see Lindbekk 1998) confirmed that the trend of the 1990s was less clear than previously; in the 1992 higher education recruitment (OLS regression analysis) there were class impact increases even in the case of the men (but the odds rates indicated a continuation of the previous trend).

Reform effects or period trend?

Our next question is if the (weakened) equalization trend that appeared for the cohort born 1964-65, was due to the educational reforms of the 1960s and 1970s, or if it was linked to changes outside the educational system? In chapters 4 and 5 some effects of the (lower) secondary education reforms appeared: the regime change from a selective («realskole») regime to a comprehensive («youth school») regime brought about increases in the educational participation of women and of youth from dispersed home loca-lities. But the impacts of class background seemed stable. By the post 1970 "integrationist" youth school pattern even a contrary trends appeared: we saw an increase in the impact of parents' education.

The various *upper* secondary regimes had not that clear impacts: "progressive" (multi-programme schools) organization added a further pull to the mobilization of women, and the regime of the most central area (Oslo/Akershus) reformatizing of educational programmes within a mostly stable situation in capacity and organization) also promoted the schooling of youth from dispersed home localities. But we noted some surprising changes in impacts of educational background and class background following the more "extreme" expansion policies in the North.

These effects were not equally pervasive. Some of them only related to attainments at particular stages in the system. This especially was the case for the impacts of various upper secondary regimes: the attainment effects mostly were limited to that particular school stage. A more "comprehensive" analysis of reform effects also should take account of the equalizing of college facilities between university areas and other areas. The early reforms in lower secondary school included all the university cities; and some of the most "inaccessible" counties came in the latest phase. We therefore cannot rule out that some of the effects attributed to the lower secondary reform, reflected developments in higher education. A penetration of these matters demands a more complex analysis than those in chapters 3 to 5.

Table 7.3 show (OLS)regression coefficients and odds rates from analyses of the 1954-55 and 1964-65 cohorts. To enable a broad range of criteria for reform evaluations, we included attainment levels and upper secondary grades as well as programme completions in higher education and the numbers with higher education advanced grades. The data on advanced grades must be considered rather incomplete; as much as half the advanced grades were completed later than age 27-28.

The calculations entered these causal variables:
1) individual background factors (gender, home locality, parents' educations, professional background, working class background),
2) school regimes of the various municipalities and counties,
3) general attainment changes for the various background categories,
4) general attainment changes in municipalities and counties with various regimes, and
5) interactions between regime/reform and individual background categories.

Among a large number of regime*background factor interactions, we focus on those with consistent or significant attainment impacts according to our previous analyses. In addition we enter "district locality" into the calculations (= counties who were targets for the new higher education policies of the 1970s. This means: all counties except the (five) with universities).

These interactions policy*background were assumed to catch attainment improvements or decreases for particular categories of youth, who had regime changes during the period that separate the two cohorts. These regime effects are considered:

A. Regime effects relating to *women's* attainments:
-By Change from selective lower secondary regime(«realskole») to comprehensive regime (« youth school»)
-By Change from a no secondary school regime to one with comprehensive lower secondary school («youth school»).
- By progressive (multi-programme) upper secondary school

- By reformatizing of programmes within the confines of
stable secondary school capacity, "average" school organization
and "academic" dominance (= the Oslo-Akershus area)
- By reformatizing of programmes combined with very large
- By large expansion of upper secondary school facilities (= the two
  Northern counties)
- By origin in area "hit" by "district" higher education policies.

B. Policies that who influenced the attainment of youth from *dispersed home localities*:
  - By change from selective to comprehensive lower secondary school regime
  - By change from a no sec.school to comprehensive lower secondary school regime
  - By origin in area "hit" by "district" higher education policies.

C. Policies that influenced the *educational background impacts:*
  - By change from selective to comprehensive lower secondary school regime
  - By change from a no sec.school regime to comprehensive lower secondary
  school regime
  - By expansive upper secondary policy (= the North area).
  - By origin in area "hit" by "district" higher education policies.

D. Policies that changed the impact of *class background:*
  - By change from selective to comprehensive lower secondary school
  regime.

 - By change from no sec. school regime to comprehensive lower secondary school
  regime.
  -By reformatizing of programmes within the confines of stable upper secondary
  capacity," average" upper secondary organization and "academic" dominance.
  -By origin in an area "hit" by "district" higher education policies.

Thus, altogether seventeen policy impacts on "distributions" were
considered.

Table 7.3 shows the regression coefficients from these rather complex
calculations, that are particularly relevant for our inquiery: Presented are
first the (OLS) regression coefficients and logistic odds rates that relate to
the general *"period"* changes (from the 1954-55 cohort to the 1964-65
cohort) for various *background factor* impacts. Thereafter are presented the
changes in impacts of *individual background* factors due to particular
policies. Coefficients for the various control variables are not given. A
more complete overview of coefficients is given in Appendix II, that relates
to the numbers who completed a higher education programme (included
there are even all the control variables).

A note of reservation for tables 7.3 and AII: We mainly want to establish if our previous conclusions about reform effects are so robust that they survive an extended analysis, where «other» school stages as well as the «causes» outside of the educational system have claimed their part. But an analysis that leaves out some "causes" that just had very small or quite inconsistent impacts (according to previous analyses), may produce the outcome that the net effect of "neglected" factors are attributed to the unspecified "period" factor.

We divide the argument into two: first we consider the large changes in attainment impacts of gender and home locality during the period: Were they caused by the extraneous «period» factor or by particular policies? After that we observe the impacts of class and educational background. The «sum» of changes here was close to zero. Was that because the «causes» we studied, were of little relevance, or did these causes counter each other?

We observe: behind the mobilization of women and youth from dispersed population areas were large, consistent and statistically significant *«period»* changes. But some of the *regime* changes contributed to these mobilizations: the changes were especially large when lower secondary comprehensive schools («youth schools») were established in municipalities that previously had no secondary facilities. And the new regime in the Oslo/Akershus area (stable capacity, average organization patterns, "academic" emphasis + new programme formats) mobilized more women.

Table 7.3. Educational Attainment Changes from 1954-55 cohort to 1964-65 cohort. Redistributions of Background Impacts Outputs from (OLS)regression analysis and odds ratio analysis.

	Attainm. level (reg. coeff.)	Gymnas grades (reg. coeff.)	Higher educ.ex. (reg. coeff.)	Advanc. grades (reg. coeff.)	Higher educ.ex (odds rates)
GEN. PERIOD CHANGE	-0.10s	3.6s	-1.2	-1.2	0.85s
Period change in background impacts:					
Per.*women	0.62s	7.5s	8.2s	3.3s	1.68s
Per.*dispersed popul.area	0.26s	4.4s	0.7	1.1	1.09
Per.*educ.background	-0.19s	-2.3s	-0.7	-4.5s	0.97
Per.*prof. class	-0.23s	-4.9	0.5	-7.7s	0.96
Per.*working class	0.03	-	1.2	1.0	1.15

Regime-caused changes in impacts of background factors					
Women*R.sk68	-0.03	0.4	1.1	-0.2	1.05
Women*Fo.sk68	0.28s	10.1s	3.0	0.8	1.37s
Women*prog.pol.	0.02	1.8	1.7	-1.2	1.09
Women*C.area	0.12	6.8s	4.5	-0.2	1.21
Women*Nor.area	-0.15	0.4	-3.6	-2.3	0.97
Woman*District	-0.11	-1.0	-3.2	-1.4	0.84
Disp.pop* Realskole68	-0.01	0.3	-1.0	-0.3	1.07
Disp.pop.* Folkeskole68	0.26	6.6s	3.5	0.7	1.37
Disp.pop* District	-0.01	-2.6	1.5	0.4	1.01
Educ.backgr* rsk->youth sch.	0.03	1.7	2.2	1.0	1.10
Educ.backgr.*no sec.->y.sch.	0.05	3.0	1.9	1.0	1.10
Educ.backgr.* North area	-	o.6	0.2	-	1.02
Educ.backgr*District	-0.02	-	-	-	1.00
Prof.cl*R.sk68	0.25	2.4	5.7s	1.5	1.18
Prof.cl*fo.sk68	-0.28	-6.3s	-7.5	-1.1	0.74
Prof.cl*C.area	-0.12	-1.0	-5.4	1.1	0.74
Prof.cl*District	-0.01	1.9	-2.7s	-0.2	0.85
Wo.cl.*R.sk68	0.18	2.2	3.2	1.5	1.11
Wo.cl.*Fo.sk68	-0.17	-9.8s	-1.0	-0.8	1.o9
Wo.cl.*C.area	-0.28	-10.7s	-3.1	-0.3	0.50s
Wo.cl.*district	0.23	3.4	-1.6	1.9	0.90s

Note to table 7.3: Coefficients for pre-reform distributions and for interactions between pre-reform attainments and regime are not included in this table. S=statistical significant effect on o.o5 level.

than men. The other policies mattered little.

We then look at the more complex issue: the seemingly «frozen» situation for impacts of class and educational background?

We first observe clear «period» factors in disfavour of "extra" attainments among youth from professional background or whose parents had much educational "capital". This period trend, as shown in table 7.3, is consistent: and five of the attainment coefficients are statistically significant. We also see that all the attainment coefficients for working class youth are positive or zero. This implies that the attainment *differences* between professional and working class background shrank according to all our period indicators.

For the *regime* factors, a more heterogeneous picture appears. a) The introduction of lower secondary comprehensive school increased the impact of *educational* background. This effect appears whether the previous regime was one with a selective lower secondary school in the municipality or the municipality had no secondary school. These regime effects appear consistently in the table, but they are small, and none of them is statistically significant. The case therefore is one where two effects countered each other, so that the net outcome became small. b) For youth from *professional* background the effects of an introduction of lower secondary comprehensive school varied. The change from selective to comprehensive lower secondary school produced an *advance* for «professional» youth group. When the previous regime was one with *no* secondary facilities in the municipality, the new comprehensive regime produced a setback for the "professionals". c) Similar trends appeared for *working class* youth. d) However, no consistent trend appeared in the attainment differences *between* the two classes, they neither widened nor decreased. We therefore may conclude: while the period trend furthered class equalization, the policies were neutral for class equalization.

Some other regime factors were more potent. While the upper secondary regime of the Oslo/Akershus area (reformatizing, academic dominance within the confines of stable capacity and "average" school organization) furthered the educational mobilization of women, it produced a significant setback for working class youth, especially for upper secondary grades.

The conclusions from the combined analysis in table 7.3 are in some cases *different* from those in previous chapters, where developments at particular school stages were considered separately. a) The gender impact by the introductions of comprehensive schools in municipalities who formerly had no secondary school, was much larger than shown in chapter 4. b) Underestimate were also the attainment gains by this reform for youth from Dispersed population areas. c) But the women's attainment gains by change from selective lower secondary regime to comprehensive regime were much smaller than previously shown.

Effects as intended.

We now may sum up the effects of the various educational regimes/changes from a point of view of the attainment redistribution that often were in the minds of the reformers.

*   The change from a selective lower secondary school regime to one with comprehensive organization (=youth school) was associated with just very small changes in attainment differences between professionalsional and working class. But both these classes had attainment advances in relation to youth from other occupational backgrounds (=intermediate strata or families that were not asso-associated with particular occupations).

*   In the municipalities that formerly had no secondary school facilities, the introduction of comprehensive lower secondary schools ("youth schools") brought about remarkable mobilizations of women and youth from dispersed home localities. These effects especially especially related to upper secondary grades. Also observed were some minor gains for youth from other strata than professions and working class.

*   The restributional effects by multi-lined organization in upper secondary school were small and inconsistent.

*   When the reformatizing of upper secondary programmes were carried out within the context examplified in the Oslo-Akershus area, the number of women who completed upper secondary grade education increased (compared with those of men), while those of working class youth declined.

*   The «district» policies in higher education (= college expansion in counties with no university) were mostly neutral from the point of view of attainment redistribution. However, in higher education some minor - negative - attainment impacts for women appeared, for youth from professional and working class background, and some advances for youth from dispersed home localities.Only the attainment advance of youth from professional backgrounds was statistically significant.

More generally: Table 7.3 reveals a more labile picture of class and educational background impacts than shown in the Shavit & Blossfeldt studies. Observed were both consistent period trends in the impacts of these factors (towards impact decreases) and regime factors that in some cases impeded these trends.

*****

8

A NEW ANALYTICAL APPROACH FOR POST-2000?

Main issue in this chapter is if data on family patterns and intra-generational mobility make for other conclusions on background factor impacts.

A more fluent society.

Conclusions from previous chapters: Equalization of educational attainments proceeded even in the 1980, and related to class backgrounds as well as gender and home localities. But it doubtful if this trend lasted into the 1990s.

But these conclusions may have been based upon a research design that was not up to the conditions of the society of today. It presumed a stability of individual background conditions that may be passè. The Western societies of the 1990s had much mobility: relating to occupations, educations, incomes as well as geographical localities and family patterns. Valid assessments of attainment patterns should consider family careers (relating to class, geographical localities as well as family forms) rather than positions and conditions at one particular time.

For the 1964-65 cohort our background data relate to 1970 - as well as 1980-conditions. They may elucidate these issues. They show the conditions of this cohort at age 6 (alternatively: age 5) and age 16 (alternatively: 15). By this we both may review the amount of stability of conditions and the attainment differences between youth from stable and mobile families.

Table 8.1. Intra-generational Class Mobility 1970 to 1980. Background Families of 1964-65 cohort.

1970 class	1980 class				Sum
	Profes- sional	Inter- mediate	Working class	No class	
Professional	16.6	2.9	0.5	1.3	21.3
Intermediate	7.0	12.6	2.4	2.2	24.1
Working class	6.0	17.4	17.8	5.5	46.6
No class	1.0	2.4	1.2	2.5	8.0
Sum	31.4	35.2	21.9	11.5	100.0

Note: the families are classified by the occupation of the higher-ranking parent.

Position changes

The class mobility figures in table 8.1 does not give a complete view of class mobility more generally, the figures just relate to the segment that was occupied by the parents of this particular cohort. Families with many children here count twice, those with no children are not included at all. However, our current object is the mechanisms that steered the inheritance of social positions (by way of educational recruitment).

Table 8.1 shows that the class mobility (during the period from young adult to middle age was large), at least among the part of the population that was integrated in society to such an extent that they founded families and got children. 53 per cent of the families changed class during this ten-year period. But the table also shows that the changes i class position were not evenly distributed. Most of the families who were "professional" in 1970, were professionals even in 1980 (16.3 per cent out of a total of 21.3 per cent). But half the "intermediates" left their 1970 "class" in the course of these years: some of them turned into professionals; a similar number entered manual work or went out of job. Most of the working class families of 1970 left that class within 1980; some of them were then out of work, but a much larger proportion was intermediates or professionals.

A more refined classification would have shown even more class mobility. However, along the line of Payne (2000) it might be argued that our entire class design is false, the class structure should rather be envisioned as one with a huge middle class that includes professionals as well as workers, delimited on the one side by one small minority (about 1 percent) of super-rich , on the other side by another minority (2 to 5 percent?) of "really" poor people. By this procedure, the main impression probably would be that the class mobility was small.

We have not conducted a special study of *the income developments* of these families. However, foreign data support that the income mobility was large around 1990. This especially related to persons in the lower brackets; most of those who were among the lowest ten percent one particular year, left that income bracket the next year (Strengmann-Kuhn 1996).

But our data on background conditions 1970 and 1980 do not support that all background conditions were in flux. 90 per cent of the members of the 1964-65 cohort belonged to the same family type in 1980 as in 1979: they either were single parent families (both years), or families with two parents both years (cohabitants or married couples). The families' "educational capital" (sum of parents' educations beyond obligatory) also was stable: 92 per cent of the cohort members came from families with the same score for educational status in 1980 as in 1970 (in relation to the four step classification used in tables 6.1 and   6.2).

Attainment impacts of family`s position changes.

The 1964-65 cohort belongs to a time when the new "fluency" was just in starting. We observed that intra-generational class mobility was frequent, but the family patterns and the families' cultural resources were even in that period stable.   But, despite that the amount of mobility varied, by the criterion used, it is worth the while to see how position changes 1970 to 1980 fed into the educational careers of the youth. The trends revealed may relate to larger numbers in the future.

Table 8.2A shows attainment impacts of family (class) mobility between childhood (1970) and youth (1980). We first observe the figures relating to the "stable" families, - along the diagonal (top left to bottom right). An average of 2.5 years of educational attainment separate "stable" professional families (1970 to 1980) from stable working class. The numbers who completed higher education programmes were 51 percent and 11.5 per cent in these «stable» categories, which makes for a net difference of 40 per cent between the two classes.

These differences should be compared with those in table 7.1; where attainments by (family) class position 1980 were considered (no differentiation between mobile and stationary families). In that table the average attainment level difference between professional class and manual working class was 1.5 years; the higher education difference between these classes was 26 per cent. - Implication: The "class" differences in table 7.1, which did not consider parent-mobility, "under-reported" the class effect by about two fifths; which is rather much.

However, when we look at youth from upward mobile families   (working class to professional class), the offspring got a doubling of higher education numbers and one extra attainment year. The "declassed" at the same time halved their higher education numbers and shortened their average attain-ment levels by half a year. Implication: for those who "stayed on" in their class, the class impacts were considerable, but at the same time, the oppor-tunities for class mobility were large,   and the impacts of the parents' mobility (on the youths` educational attainments) became large as well.

For educational background the mobility-corrected picture was different. The attainment figures along the diagonal (relating to families with stable educational "capital")differed little from those found when just educational status 1980 was considered. Educational background, clearly is a more robust causal factor than class.   Even large educational demotions (commonly: because one parent with much educational "capital" left the family) were not associated with "attainment falls" for the offspring.

Table 8C shows clear attainment differences between youth from stable two parent families and youth from families who either in 1970 or in 1980   (or

Table 8.2A. Attainment Effects of Family's Class Mobility 1970 to 1980.

1970 class	1980 class			
	Profes-sional	Inter-mediate	Working class	No class
	Attainment level:			
Profession	13.2	12.4	11.6	11.8
Intermediate	12.2	11.9	11.4	11.3
Working class	12.0	11.5	11.2	11.0
No class	12.6	11.4	10.7	11.1
:	Higher Education:			
Professional	50.8	34.5	20.4	17.8
Intermediate	31.9	24.8	15.7	10.4
Working class	22.8	18.3	13.0	5.8
No class	39.5	21.1	11.5	11.3

Table 8.2B. Attainment Effects of Family's Educational Mobility 1970 to 1980.

Education status 1970	Educ. status 1980			
	5-6	4	3-2	1-0
Attainment level:				
5 - 6 (high)	13.7	13.2	13.1	13.9
4	13.2	13.0	12.6	12.8
3 - 2	12.6	12.7	12.2	12.0
1 - 0 (low)	11.9	11.7	11.6	11.2
Higher educat.:				
5 - 6 (high)	61.5	53.0	47.9	61.5
4	52.1	47.2	35.7	43.8
3 - 2	43.8	42.2	30.7	29.8
1 - 0 (low)	20.3	15.1	14.6	13.5

Table 8.2C. Attainment Effects of Changes
in Family Composition 1970 to 1980.

Family type 1970	Family type 1980	
	Two parents	Other family
	Attainment level:	
Two parents	11.77	11.26
Other family	10.78	11.18
	Higher education:	
Two parents	22.7	15.6
Other family	9.1	15.2

both years) had just one parent. It also appears that the 1970 family type counted more for attainments than that ten years later. The largest attainment differences by family type appeared between "stable" two-parent families and the single parent families of 1970 who "added" one more parent in 1980.

The attainment differences between family types were large, between youth from stable two-parent families and youth from families who had just one parent at the outset, the average attainment level differences made up one year in attainment levels, and the higher education rate difference was thirteen percent.

When we compare the attainment difference in table 8C with those in tables 8.2A and 8.2B, we observe that the differences by family type equaled the size of those by class, and they were half those by extreme differences in educational background. We shall return to these issues in the sections below, which are devoted to presentation of the outputs from multi-variat regression analyses.

Attainment as a function of position-changes 1970-1980

Into (OLS) regressions and ODDS RATIO-analyses of attainments were entered the background factors employed in tables 8A-C. In addition to that: home locality 1970 and 1980, number of siblings (1970), and if the mother was occupationally active (outside of the home) in 1970 or 1980. The analysis by this extended from just "macro"-factors to one that included some important micro factors, relating to the youth and childhood periods.

Table 8.3. Attainment impacts of Background Conditions and Background Condition Changes. (OLS) regression coefficients and Odds Ratios.1964-65 cohort.

Background conditions	Attainm.lev. Higher ed		Higher educaton : Odds ratio
	Reg.coef.	Reg.coef	
Impact of 1970 conditions:			
Professional class	0.910s	16.6s	2.57s
Intermediate class	0.540s	7.7s	1.78s
No class	0.210	5.3s	1.51s
(Ref cat: Working class)			
Father's education	0.318s	5.3s	1.38s
Mother's education	0.340s	6.8s	1.38s
(educ. levels from 0 to 4)			
Large city	-0.092	-	1.00
Dispersed pop area	-0.040	0.7	1.03
(Ref. cat.: small town/ other densely pop area)			
Mother occup. active	-0.001	1.2	1.09
Two-parent family	0.253s	2.9	1.21
Number of children in the family: four or more.	-0.028	0.5	1.02
Effect of changes 1970-1980:	Att.level	Higher ed. perc.	Higher ed.
Prof.class->other position	0.447	-11.3s	0.63s
Other pos->prof class	0.208	2.7	1.21s
Interm.pos->working class or no class	0.280s	-5.5s	0.69s
Working class or no class-> Interm.position	0.193	1.6	1.18
No class->working class	0.310	4.8s	1.32s
(Ref.cat: stably work.class)			
Educational adv.father	0.028	-3.8	0.89
	0.306	4.1	

Educational adv.mother	-0.021	2.5	1.29
Educat.adv. sum parents			1.10
(Ref.cat.:Stable educ.status)	-0.084	0.4	
Large city, stable	-0.093	-3.7	
Largecity->densely pop. Area	-0.384	-6.0	1.02 / 0.80 / 0.69
Large city->disp.pop.area	-0.090	-3.2	
Densely pop.area->large city			0.80
Densely.pop.a.> .disp.pop.a.	-0.109	-2.1	
	0.321s	8.1	0.86
Disp.pop.area->large city			1.63s
Disp.pop.a->densely pop.a.	-0.079	-0.4	
	0.005	0.2	0.96 / 1.00
Disp.pop.area, stable			
(Ref.cat.:Dense area stable)	0.253s	6.5	
Two parent fam.,stable	-0.264	0.4	1.58s / 1.02
Two parent fam..>single parent			
Single parent fam.->two parent	0.007	2.6	
(Ref.cat:Single parent fam.stable)			1.23
Occ.active mother,stable	-0.010	1.2	
Occ.active mo.-> inactive	0.018	0.3	1.09 / 1.01 / 1.14
Occ.inactive mo.->active	-0.029	1.8	
(Ref.cat.:Mother.occ. inactive, stable)			

Tables 8.3 and 8.4 present the most relevant outputs from these analyses. Focused in table 8.3 is first the background impacts 1970, after that the impacts of particular "background careers" 1970 to 1980 (the general changes in attainments and in attainment impacts of particular background factors 1970 to 1980 are not shown in the table). Table 8.3 shows the "combined" figures for men and women. Table 8.4 gives separate figures for the two genders.

The upper part of Table 8.3 shows the impacts of individual background factors 1970, after the impacts of other factors are deducted. The class background figures have working class as reference. We note that the "advantages" by professional back-ground (compared with working class background) now amounts to 0.9 in average attainment level and 16.6 in higher education per cent. These differences are about two thirds those shown in Table 7.1. Interesting are the equal and large effects of the two parents` educations, and a statistically significant plus for two-parent families (which remains after the impacts of class and educational capital have been accounted for).

The next section explores the impacts of various position changes 1970 to 1980. First exhibited are those of class backgrounds. Both advancements and demotions had large and statistically significant impacts; largest were those by demotion from professional class. Large was also (the attainment gain) when at family moved from a jobless condition to working class. The data summarized in 8.4 shows that these impacts of class changes were particularly large for women.

While changes (increases) in father`s educational capital mattered little for the attainments of the offspring, the impacts of the educational activities of the mothers were more decisive.

The attainments varied little between the towns and other geographical home communities. But two (complementary) effects emerged by geographical mobility: Significant advances appeared for school careers that started in dispersed areas, and continued in large cities; also clear (but statistically not significant) losses came by mobility from large city to dispersed area. Perceivable is also: further attainment gain for youth from two-parent families who remained two-parent during the period, and equally large loss by families who now turned single-parent. Table 8.4 shows that the family patterns and the changes in family patterns were particularly large - and statistically significant - for men`s attainments, just half that large were the effects in the case of women.

The figures show no attainment impacts of the changes in the mother`s occupational activity during the period.

*****

Different research designs - different conclusions on educational recruitement?

Class background and educational capital were the most resilient of the background factors explored in chapters 3-7. The 1970 class and educational background explained 16.9 per cent of the variations in attainment levels. Class and educational background 1980 explained 16.6 per cent. For higher education the figures were around 14 per cent by both analyses.

Table 8.4. Attainment Impacts of Parent Postitions and Mobility.
Regressions coefficients. Joint and Separately for men and women.

	Attainment levels			Higher education		
	Sum	Men	Women	Sum	Men	Women
Class:						
Professional,stable	0.903s	0.757s	1.058s	16.3s	14.8s	17.9s
Lower->professional	0.459s	0.303s	0.620s	6.8s	5.4s	8.2s
Professional->lower	0.486s	0.482s	0.501s	7.9s	10.8s	4.8s
Intermediate,stable	0.658s	0.604s	0.717s	9.2s	8.6s	9.9s
Lower->intermediate	0.222s	0.109	0.347s	2.2	1.0	3.6
Intermediate->lower	0.142	0.104	0.189	1.9	1.4	2.6
(Ref.: Working class or No class both 1970 and 1980)						
Income 1980						
1 SD below average	-0.162s	-0.206s	-0.116	-2.2s	-1.8	-2.7
(Ref.:Larger income)						
Educational background:						
Parents' education 1970	0.355s	0.361s	0.347s	6.9s	7.3s	6.5s
Parents' education 1980	0.063	0.043	0.088	1.0	-0.1	2.3s
Parents, education:						
increase 1970 to 1980	0.221s	0.278s	0.151	4.1s	5.2s	2.8
(calculated in relation to 6 step variable)						
Family conditions:						
Two parents,stably	0.300s	0.417s	0.172s	3.7s	5.1s	2.0
(Ref.single parent either 1970 or 1980)						
Mother occ.active 1980	0.006	0.052	-0.042	2.0s	2.8	1.1
(Ref.:Moth not occ.active 1980)						

Home locality:						
Large city	-0.056	-0.030	-0.078	0.5	0.3	0.8
Dispersed popul.area	-0.034	-0.075	-0.078	-0.5	-1.6	0.6
(Ref.: Small town or rural density)						
Gender:						
Women	0.178			7.1		

When all the factors in tables 8.3 and 8.4 had been entered, they together explained 18.8 per cent of the variations in attainment levels, 14.5 per cent of the variations in higher education. Implication: despite the significant impacts by particular interactions (for instance by gender*family type or by class advances or class demotions 1970 to 1980) these factors were not able to explain more than a fraction of the entire attainment variation of the 1964-65 cohort.

But some more particular findings were large and worth emphasis, for theoretical and policy reasons: 1. The attainment impact of class is so sensitive to short-term class mobility that the theory of deeply ingrained class-habituses get into difficulties. 2. The attainment impact of mother's recent educational advance points at network- and motivation effects that have been little explored. Our finding have implications for current adult education policies. 3. The positive effects of school careers that started in dispersed areas and continued in large cities, actualize theories from other parts of sociology, notably immigration theories : that the newcomers found (and invested energies in) niches within the urban society, who provided opportunities for shielded advance In other words: schooling did not function as a "foreign culture" in the country-side, rather as a "pro-tected area" for rural youth, who afterwards attained further advances in the city. 4.Confirmed are previous findings that "incompleteness" of families commonly impaired the careers of the offspring. New is that we were able to calculate the long-term size of this handicap and relate it to the impacts of some other frequent types of advantage/handicap .

*****

9

OBSERVATIONS AND PERSPECTIVES

We wanted to observe the effects of a number of reforms in Norwegian education during the 1950s to 1970s. Administrative, organizational and pedagogical integration and unification were catchwords for these reforms. Intended was an educational upgrading of the population as well as equalization of opportunities. Did the reformers succeed?

We compared youths born in the mid-sixties with those who were born ten years before, and observed increases in the numbers who completed three years of upper secondary education. Observed was also that the number who completed some programme in higher education (but this growth was not large). That there was growth, is not surprising in view of the expansions in school facilities in most counties and municipalities. One may rather wonder why the number who completed educational programmes at universities and colleges did not increase more than they did. The increases in «substantial» qualifications were probably more limited than shown in the statistics for completed school stages; the instruction time per year in secondary school diminished by nearly one fifth, during the period that separates these cohorts. But the attainment advances following the introduction of lower secondary schools in municipalities previously lacking such facilities, certainly exceeded the loss of effect due to the shrinking of the school year. Notable was also the attainment increases that were produced by the decentralization policies in higher education.

However the general changes in qualification levels changed, the attainments became more *evenly distributed*. The standard deviations of attainment levels diminished. But the conclusion that an equalizing of attainments came about, must be qualified. The attainment differences by gender and home locality mostly *vanished* in this period, due to organizational changes as well as more general trends. But the very large attainment differences that reflected *social class* and the *educational capital* of the individual family, mostly remained.

The "change factors" at work in these years, implied three sets of «causes»: New patterns of school organization, extra resources for educational purposes (new schools, more teachers etc), and changes outside of the educational sector (especially in economy and welfare systems). The attainment material we have surveyed indicates that the impact of the period's organizational innovations were little impressive: neither the "consolidation" of rural primary schools nor the comprehensivization of secondary school and extension of compulsory schooling produced attainment level increases or larger numbers willing to/capable of "gymnas" grades or higher education.

However, the *redistributional* impacts of the new organization patterns were larger than the general changes in attainments. Such impacts particularly appeared by the new lower secondary school regime: a «new deal» for the women and for youth from dispersed home localities. The «unstreamed» youth school of the 1970s differed in many ways from the «lined» school of the first reform period. But the distributional effects of the two patterns of comprehensive school were mostly the same.

A much investigated issue in current educational sociology was if postwar education (for whatever reason) were distributed more "equally" between classes and cultural strata. Even though the answer generally has been yes for the early part of the postwar period, there in most countries was much doubt relating to more recent trends. The Norwegian case supports this doubt. After 1980 the trend toward larger equality of attainments between classes and cultural strata weakened, after 1990 it may have vanished altogether.

These conclusions imply that two educational theories with large political implications must be given up: relating to the impacts of an extension of compulsory schooling and of the comprehensive (as against "selective, segregated or the amount of "differentiation"") schooling. The process of ambition formation and development of reference groups evidently needs reworking. Also how resources differences influenced attainments. The attainment effects by extension of compulsory schooling were disappointing, but not those who appeared after colleges and lower secondary schools were established outside of more central school places.

*****

While there occurred an educational mobilization of the women and youth from the countryside took place following some of the regime changes, the impacts of class background and cultural capital were more constant and little sensitive to regime differences. But the class factor was more labile than commonly assumed. During the interval between 1970 and 1980, nearly half the families changed their class positions. These changes were followed large changes in the educational careers of the offspring. The women were especially sensitive to such "intra-generational" mobility. We also observed that changes in the parents' educational status, (probably due to adult education), and family patterns (especially relevant for the schooling of the boys) were important. Even though the attainment effects by «stable» class background positions were as large as previously, the combined effects changes in other matters (family pattern, amount of cultural capital, home locality) were so large that they might equal the class effect. Theses conclusions have quite different policy implications than the theory of large as well as deep-seated habitus-differences between the classes.

In contrast to some limited changes in class effects, remains the strong as well as stable impact of the families' (very different) amounts of cultural capital. One may ask to what extent this resilience reflects the successful educational policies of one period that now is just history: the firm educational hierarchies that was produced by the well-integrated school system of the first postwar period. If that is so, a weakening of the cultural background factor will appear when children from families schooled in the 1970s, appear in school..

Probable is also that urbanization and mobility will destroy the community school effect that our data indicated, which gave rural youth a lasting advantage.

*****

APPENDIX I: DESCRIPTIVE STATISTICS

A.1. Average Attainment Levels; as a function of Father's and Mother's Level of (Highest Education*. 1964-65 cohort. (N=10496)

Mother's level of highest education	Father's level of highest education				
	0	1	2	3	4
0	11.08	11.67	11.75	12.19	12.84
1	11.60	12.13	12.19	12.69	13.29
2	11.95	12.05	12.51	12.81	13.16
3	11.67	12.78	12.83	13.15	13.40
4	12.66	(13.50)	13.24	12.97	13.61

Note : Classifications of individual levels of education:
0=Just obligatory
1=Short (1-2year) secondary education
2=Completed upper secondary education
3=Short (1-3years) higher education
4=Completed university grade

A. 2. Average Attainment Levels and Percents with Higher Education Exams, by Background factors. 1954-55 cohort and 1964-65 cohort.   N=23.212

	Average att.level		Higher educ.perc.	
	Born 1954-55	Born 1964-65	Born 1954-55	Born 1964-65
Family's class:				
Professional	12.2	12.7	43.0	39.4
Intermediate	10.9	11.7	21.0	20.3
Manual work	10.4	11.2	13.5	13.0
No class	9.9	11.2	13.1	13.7
A3 (cont.)				
Family's Educ. Level:				
0-1	10.6	11.4	17.1	15.0
6-8	13.7	14.1	68.1	64.8

Locality:				
Dense popul.	13.1	11.9	25.8	26.4
Dispersed pop.	10.7	11.6	16.3	18.6
Gender:				
Men	11.4	11.8	22.5	20.4
Women	10.8	11.9	21.5	27.8
All	*11.0*	*11.9*	*22.0*	*23.9*
S.D.	*2.35*	*2.08*	-	-

A 3. Average Attainment Levels and Percent with Higher
Education,by Parents' Social Class and Parents' (combined)
Levels of Education. 1964-65 cohort.

Class backgr.	Parents' educ. level.			Parents' educ.level		
	1	2	3	4	5	6
Av.att. levels						
Prof.cl	11.99	12.06	12.72	12.68	13.46	13.61
Interm	11.77	11.92	12.30	12.64	13.16	13.50
Work.cl	11.03	11.76	11.90	11.77	11.75	-
Hig.ed.percent						
Prof.cl	26.0	29.1	39.5	40.5	57.4	63.5
Interm.	14.6	25.7	30.9	36.4	49.3	58.7
Work.cl	9.4	20.4	26.0	22.7	0	-
Samples						
Prof.cl	313	460	1710	398	319	195
Interm.	1061	796	185	205	138	40
Work.cl .	789	321	21	22	4	0

Note: each step on the parents' education variable =equals ca. .
two years of education (combined for the parents).
· Sum scores =6-8 were in   A3 given the value 6.

APPENDIX II

Attainment Developments from the 1954-55 cohort to 1964-65 cohort. Proportion with higher education exams. Detailed output from (OLS) regression analysis

FACTORS ENTERED	REGR.COEFF. (B-scores)	STANDARD ERROR	BETA COEFF.
Original background impacts:			
Women	-1.1	1.3	-0.024
Disp.home locality	-2.9	1.8	-0.032
Parents' education	12.5S	0.6	0.268
Professional class	9.3S	2.3	0.088
Working class	-3.5	1.8	-0.042
Original impacts of educational regime:			
Decentr. primary school	2.8	1.7	0.012
Realskole	5.4	4.4	0.046
No sec. school	-5.5	8.9	-0.026
Progressiv up.sec.pol.	1.6	2.6	0.013
Conservative up.sec.	-0.8	2.8	-0.007
«Central region» pol.	10.7S	1.9	o.102
«Northern region»pol.	-0.9	4.0	-0.006
«District»higher educ.	-1.8	2.8	-0.023
*Interactions regime *back-ground factor:*			
Women*realskole	-2.5	2.1	-0.016
Women*no sec.sch. .	-1.6	3.8	-0.002
Women*prog.pol.	-1.8	2.5	-0.010
Women*cons.pol	-3.2	1.5	-0.021
Women*Central region	-7.0S	1.5	-0.045
Women*Northern region	0.1	3.0	-
Women*District	0.2	1.8	0.002
Disp.loc.*realskole	0.9	2.2	0.006
Disp.loc.*no sec.sch.	-1.5	4.4	-0.006
Disp.loc*prog.pol.	0.5	1.8	0.003
Disp.area*cons.pol.	-0.7	1.7	-0.002
Disp.loc.*Centr.region	0.1	2.0	-
Disp.loc.*North.region	2.6	2.1	0.011
Disp.loc.*District	-4.7	2.0	-0.010

	-0.1	1.5	-0.003
Parents.ed.*realskole	2.3	3.2	0.026
Parents'ed.*no sec.sch.	-0.1	1.1	-0.002
Parents'ed.*prog.pol.	2.2	o.9	0.059
Parents'ed.*cons.pol.	0.8	0.6	0.023
Parents'ed*Centr.reg.	-0.9	1.4	-0.014
Parents'ed.*North.reg.	0.1	0.9	0.005
Parents'ed.*District	-	3.0	-
Prof.class*realskole	1.9	4.1	0.002
Prof.class*no sec.sch.	-	2.8	0.001
Prof.class*prog.pol	-3.7	2.5	-0.016
Prof.class*cons.pol.	-3.3	3.7	-0.016
Prof.class*Centr.region	0.4	3.1	0.001
Prof.class*North.region	8.2	3.1	0.060
Prof.class*District	-2.7	2.3	-0.017
Working cl.*realskole	2.4	4.0	0.007
Working cl.*no sec.sch.	1.9	2.0	0.011
Working cl.*prog.pol.	-1.4	1.8	-0.009
Working cl.*cons.pol.	-5.6	2.5	-0.034
Working cl.*Centr.reg.	-4.6S	2.4	-0.022
Working cl.*North.reg.	-3.3	2.1	-0.036
Working cl.*District			
Period changes: attainm.effects of background:			
Women	8.2S	2.1	0.084
Dispersed localities	0.7	2.1	0.006
Parents'education	-0.7	0.8	-0.027
Professional class	0.5	1.4	0.004
Working class	1.2	2.5	0.012
Period effects: attainm.effects of regime:			
Realskole->youth sch.	-10.4	6.3	-0.065
No sec.sch-> youth sc.	- 3.0	12.7	-0.007
Progressive up.sec.pol.	- 1,1	2.5	-0.006
Conserv.up.sec.policy	0.8	1.6	0.002
Central region policy	- 7.6S	3.0	-0.051
Northern region pol.	0.6	3.0	-0.002
District policy	4.1	3.6	0.041
Background changes in attainment as functions of			

policies:			
Women by r.sk->y.sch.	1,1	3.0	0.004
Women by no sec>y.sc.	3.0	5.5	0.027
Women by prog.sec.pol.	1.7	3.5	0.007
Women by Centr.reg.pol	4.5	2.9	0.022
Women by North.r.pol.	-3.6	4.1	-0.012
Women by District pol.	-3.2	2.7	-0.028
Disp.loc.by rsk->ysch.	1.0	2.5	0.004
Disp.loc.by no.sec-> youth school	3.5	6.3	0.010
Disp.loc.by Distr.pol.	1.5	2.5	0.011
Parents'educ. by realsk->youth s.	2.2	2.0	0.038
Parents' educ by no sec.->y.sch.	1.9	4.4	0.016
Parents' educ by District pol.	-	-	0.020
Prof.class by realsk. ->youth school	5.7	3.7	0.016
Prof.class by no sec. ->youth school	-7.5	9.4	-0.009
Prof.class by Central region policy	-5.4	3,7	-0.023
Prof.class by District policy	-15.0S	2.8	0.100
Working cl. by realsk ->youth school	3.2	3.4	0.014
Working cl. by no sec. ->youth school	1.0	6.2	0.002
Working cl. by Central region policy	-3.1	3.8	-0.011
Working cl. by District Policy	-1.6	2.8	0.013
Constant	-4.6	2.0	

S=statistically significant effect on 0.05 level
Reference categories were:
    for women: men
    for disp.home localities: densely pop.localities
    for prof.& work.class : Other backgrounds
    for realskole & no sec.school: youth school regime

    for progressive & conservative up.sec.policies:
        other regime

for Central & Northernregions' policies: policies of
other regions
for District position in higher education policies:
policies for university areas

REFERENCES

Atkinson,P., 1985: *Language, Structure and Reproduction.London,*
Methuen.

Aubert,V., Haldorsen,G. and Tiller,P.O. 1956: Lærernes holdning
til yrkesrollen og oppdragelsesspørsmål. *Norsk pedagogisk*
tidsskrift, 3, pp 90-99.

Aubert,V., 1960: Norske jurister fra 1814 til den annen
verdenskrig. Oslo, Institutt for samfunnsforskning,
(mimeo).

Bellaby,P., 1977: *The Sociology of Comprehensive*
Schooling. London, Methuen.

Bernstein,B, 1969: "Social Class and Linguistic Development",
in: Halsey,H.H.(ed.): *Education, Economy and Society.,*
Glencoe, Free Press pp.288-314.

Blake, J.,1989: *Family Size and Achievement.* Univ.of California
Press.

Blau, P.M. and Duncan, O.D., 1967: *The American Occupational*
Structure, New York.

Bonesrønning,H.,1996: "School Characteristics and Student
Achievement. Evidence from Combined Upper Secondary
Schools in Norway",*Educational Economics* 4:2, pp.143-160.

Bourdieu,P.andPasserons, J.C., 1977: *Reproduction: In Society,*
Society, and Culture. California, Beverley.

Bourdieu,P.,1989:*Distinction,*London, Routledge.

Breen, R. and Goldthorpe, J.H., 1996: "Class (and Gender)
Differentials in Educational Attainment: Towards a formal
theory." Stockholm, ISA, Group 28 Research Conference
(mimeo).

Coleman,J.S. et al.,1966: *Equality of Education Opportunity,*
Washington D.C., Government Printing office.

Coombs, 1985: *The World Crisis in Education.* London, Macmillan

Dahlløf,U., 1990: *Changes within the Swedish School*
System and Their Effects. In Leschinsky, A. and
Mayer,K.U., eds: The Comprehensive School Experiment
Revisited, Frankfurt, Peter Lang, pp.174-211.

Darnell,F. and Hoem, A. 1996: *Taken into the Extremes. Education and the Far North.* Oslo, Scandinavian University Press.

Deeben, R. 1968: On What is Learned in School. New York, Addison-Wesley.

Det norske samfunn (ed.:N.Rogoff Ramsøy), 1968, Oslo, Gyldendal.

Duru-Bellah and Mingat,A 1990: How do French Junior Secondary Schools Operate? in eds.: Leschinsky, A. and Mayer, K.U.: *The Comprehensive School Experiment Revisited,* Frankfurt, P.Lang, pp.62-91.

Erikson,R. and Jonsson,J., 1983: *Ursprung och utbildning.* Stockholm, SOU 1993:85, Utbildningsdepartementet.

Erikson,R. and Jonsson,J. 1996: *Can Education be Equalized?* Stockholm, Westview Press.

Erikson R. and Jonsson, J., 1994: *Sorteringen i skolan.* Stockholm, Carlssons.

Esping-Andersen,G. "Mobility Regimes and Class Formation", in: Esping-Andersen,G. (ed.): *Changing Classes, Statification and Mobility in Postindustrial Societies.* London etc. Sage, pp225-241.

Falck,T. and Rattsø,J., 1995: *The Politics of Resource Use in High Schools".* Trondheim, Dept. of Economics(mimeo).

Forsøksrådets melding 1955/56, Oslo, Forsøksrådet for skoleverket.

Fuligni, A. 1997: The Academic Achievement of Adolescents from Immigrant Families: The Roles of Family Background, Attitudes and Behavior, *Child Development,* 68:2, pp 351-363.

Funksjonshemmede i samfunnet, 1977-78. *Stortingsmelding nr. 23 1977-78.,* Oslo, Sosialdepartementet.

Fürst, E., 1988: *Kvinner i Akademia - inntrengere i en mannsbastion.* Oslo, NAVFs sekretariat for kvinneforskning.

Gamoran, A., 1993: *Curriculum Standardization and Equality of Opportunity in Scottish Secondary Education.* Paper to ISA Conference Research Committee 28, Trondheim.

Gjesme,T. 1994: Grouping in Education and Motivation. 88, *Scandinavian Educational Research,*pp.245-265.

Goldthorpe J.H. et al. 1980: *Social Mobility and Class Structure in Modern Britain.* Oxford, Clarendon Press.

Gooderham,P, Lindbekk, T, og Ringdal,K., 1993: Translation of The Erikson-Goldthorpe Scale. *ISS-RAPPORT,* 41. Trondheim

de Graaf, P. and Ganzeboo,H. 1992. Family Background and Educational Achievement in Netherlands for the 1891-1960 Birth Cohorts. in eds. Shavitt,Y. and Blossfeld,H.P.: *Persistent Inequalities,* Boulder etc. Westview Press, pp.75-100.

Gray, J., 1990: Has Comprehensive School Succeeded?
In Leschinsky,A and Mayer,K.U.,eds.: *The Comprehensive School* Experiment Revisited, Frankfurt, P.Lang, pp.111-138.

Green,A. 1990: *Education and State Formation.* London, Macmillan.

Grøgaard, J.B.1992: Skomaker bli ved din lest. *FAFO-notat.*Oslo.

Halinan, M.L., 1994: Tracking : from Theory to Practice. *Sociology of Education.* 2, p.79-89.

Hanushek,E.A., Rivkin, S.G. and Taylor, L.L.,1994: *Aggregation and the Estimated Effect of School Resources,* Working Pater no 397, Washington D.C., University of Rochester (Mimeo).

Hargreaves,D.H. 1967: *Social relations in a Secondary School* London, Routledge and Kegan Paul.

Hargreaves,D.H. 1982: *The Challenge for the Comprehensive School. Routledge and Kegan Paul.*

Havemann, R. and Wolfe, B.,1995: "The Determinants of Children's Attainments". A Review of Methods and Findings",*Journal of Economic Literature*, 33:pp.1829-1878.

Head start. Eds. Zigler, E. and Muenchow, S., 1994. Basic Books, New York

Hernes G, and Knudsen K. 1976: Utdanning og ulikhet *NOU,* 1976:46. Oslo, Universitetsforlaget

Hoem, A., 1976: *Makt og kunnskap,* Oslo, Universitetsforlage.

Hout, N., 1989: *Following in Father's Footsteps,* Harvard Univ.Press.

Haavelsrud, M. 1984: *Perspektiver i utdanningssosiologi,* Oslo, Universitetsforlaget.

Ingebrigtsen, O.,1982: *Videregående skoler 1960-1980,* Statistikk og analyser. 1-4. Trondheim, Institutt for sosiologi og samfunnskunnskap.

Innstilling fra Samordningsnemda for skoleverket, Sammenfatning og utsyn. Mysen. Indre Smaalenenes trykkeri.

Iversen, G.,1971: *Utdanningssøkning og evneutnytting blant et årskull unge menn.* Oslo, Institutt for anvendt sosialvitenskapelig forskning (mimeo).

Jackson,B. and Marsden, D., 1962:*Education and the Working Class,*London, Routledge and Kegan Paul.

Jonsson,J.,1990: Educational reform and Changes in Inequality in Sweden. In Eds. Leschinsky, A. and Mayer,K.U.: *The Comprehensive School Experiment Revisited* Frankfurt, P.Lang, pp 139-173.

Karlsen,G., 1993: *Desentralisert skoleutvikling,* Oslo, Ad Notam.

Kerkhof, A.C., 1993: The Secondary School reform: The More Things Change......, *ISA Reseach Committee 28.* Trondheim (mimeo).

Knudsen, K. 1976: *Ulikhet i grunnskolen*, Oslo, Universitetsforlaget

Knudsen,K., Sørensen, Aa.B., Aamodt, P.P., 1993: *Endringen i
den sosiale rekrutteringen til høyere utdanning etter
1980*, Notat, Oslo, NAVFs utrednings-institutt

Kohn, M.,1969: *Class and Conformity*, Homewood, Dortesy Press.

Krange,O.and Bakken, A. 1998: Innvandrerungdoms skole-
prestasjoner. *Tidsskrift for samfunnsforskning*, 3.pp381-
410.

Kyvik, S. 1980: *Desentralisering av høgre utdanning og
forskning. NAVFs utredningsinstitutt, Utredninger* 1980:2.
Oslo

Laukli, O., 1954: " *Miljø og skoleframgang*", Forskning og
danning,1, pp.115.

Lauglo, J., 1997: *Working Harder to Make the Grade. Immigrant
Youth in Norwegian Schools. (forthcoming)*.

Lechinsky, A. and Mayer, K.U., 1990: The Comprehensive
School and and Inequality of Opportunity in the Federal
republic of Germany. In *The Comprehensive School
Experiment Revisited (Eds. by Leschinsky, A. and Mayer,
K.U.)*, Frankfurt, P. Lang, pp 13-37.

Lindbekk,T. 1969; *Ecological Factors and the Attainment
Process*. In Education in Europe, Eds.: C.Vervoord and
M.Matthijssen, Hague,Houton, pp.13.23.

Lindbekk,T., 1962: *De lærde profesjoner i Norge*, Oslo, Institutt for samfunnsforskning .
(mimeo)

Lindbekk,T., 1968: "Den niårige skolen som demokratiserende
faktor", *Norsk pedagogisk tidsskrift*.

Lindbekk,T., 1994: Repetisjoner og nedadgående løp. *Iss-
rapport*, 39/1994, Trondheim.

Lindbekk,T., 1979: Skoleutvikling og utdanningsutbytte
i perioden 1945-1955. In Ed.:Lindbekk,T.: *Samfunnsendring*,
Trondheim, Tapir, pp 119-144.

Listhaug,O. et al., 1982: Status attainment in rural and urban
labour markets. *Acta Sociologica*, 25,2:269-282.

Lysgaard, S., 1961: *Arbeiderkollektivet*, Oslo, Universitetsforlaget.

Mannsåker, D., 1954: Det norske presteskapet i det
19.hundreåret.Oslo, Universitetsforlaget.

Marklund,S., 1984: Sweden. In ed.: Hough, J.: *Educational
Policy* London, St.Martins Press.

Mogstad,L.1958: Et tilskott til klarlegging av sentraliserings-
spørsmålet i landsfolkeskulen. *Forsking og danning*, 3.

Mortimore et al., 1989: *School Matters; The Junior
Years*. Somerset, Open Book

Myklebust, J.O., 1972:   Skulen i lokalkulturen, *Trondheim-studier i skolesosiologi*. Trondheim,Tapir

Nilsson, L., 1981: *Yrkesutbildning i nutidshistoriskt perspektiv*, Gøteborg, Acta universitatis Gothobergensis

Norsk skole, 1958-1980. Oslo, utgitt av Kirke- og undervisnings-departementet.

Nørstebø, S., 1962: Preliminarister og "norsk" embetseksamen. Oslo, Universitetsforlaget.

OECD, 1985: *Education and Training after Basic Schooling.* Paris, OECD.

Om grunnskolen, 1982.: *St.melding nr. 62, 1982-83.* Oslo, Kirke-og undervisningsdepartementet.

Om videregående opplæring, 1984: *St.meld. nr.15 1984-1985*, Oslo. Kirke- og undervisningsdepartementet

Om høgre utdanning, 1984: *St.meld. nr.66, 1984-85.* Kirke- og undervisningsdepartmentet.

Palmstrøm, H. 1936: "En akademikergruppe gjennom hundre år," *Statsøkonomisk tidsskrift.*

Pappas, Aa. et al.,1994:   Ability-Group Effects, in Education. 141/1994, p.27-46.

Payne.G.2000: *Social Divisions*. London,MacMillan

Pedersen,W., 1996:"Marginalitetens reproduksjon". Tidsskrift for samfunnsforskning, 37, pp.3-23.

Persistent Inequality, 1993, eds: Shavitt, M. and Blossfeld, H.P. Colorado, Westview Press.

Prost, A., 1990: Schooling and Social Stratification. Paradoxes of the Reform of the middle school in 20th Century France. In Lescinsky, A., and Mayer, K.U. eds: *The Comprehensive School Experiment Revisited*,, Frankfurt, P.Lang, pp 38-61

Resultater og erfaringer fra Regjeringens handlingsplan for funksjonshemmede og veien videre. *St.meld.nr.34, 1996-97.*

Riksaasen, S.1989: *Grunnskolen, et systemn i krise.*Oslo, Gyldendal.

Rogoff Ramsøy, N., 1977: *Sosial mobilitet i Norge*, Oslo, Tiden.

Rust, D., 1989: *The Democratic Tradition and the Evolution of Schooling in Norway*. London, Greenwood.

Rutter, M. 1983:   School Effects on Pupils' Progress. *Cild Development.* Vol.54, no.1:1-29.

Salter, B. and Tapper, T., 1985: *Power and Policy in Education*, The Case of the Independent Sector.Barcombe, Falmer Press.

Shavitt,Y. and Blossfeld, H.P., 1992: *Persistent Inequality, Changing Educational Stratification in Thirteen Countries.* Boulder etc, Westview Press.

Similä, M., 1994: Andra generationens innvandrare i den svenska

skolan. In: eds. Erikson,R. and Jonsson, J.J.:
Sorteringen i skolan, Stockholm, Carlssons.

Sirevåg, T. 1979: *Den niårige skolen i opphav og strid*. Oslo, Aschehoug.

Skolens årbok, 1965-1968, Oslo.

Slagstad, R., 1994.: Arbeiderpartiet som skolestat. *Nytt norsk tidsskrift*, 3-4

Stafseng, O., 1996: *Den historiske konstruksjon av moderne ungdom*, Oslo, Cappelen akademisk forlag.

Strengmann-Kuhn,W., 1996: "Labour Market Participation of the Labour Market Participation of the Poor in West Germany". Berlin, Paper for the ECSR Workshop,August 26-27.,

Strømnes, M., 1947: *Tidsskifte i landsfolkeskolen, Oslo, Aschehoug*.

Sunde, R. and Vestby, E. 1969: "Avgangsprøva ved små ungdomsskoler.To undersøkelser". *Forsøksrådets informasjonsserie*, 5, pp.42-53.

Sørensen, R., 1995: *Local Government School Priorities,* Oslo, Norwegian School of Management. (mimeo).

Telhaug,A.O., 1975: *Vår nye videregående skole*. Oslo, Lærerstudentenes forlag.

Telhaug,A.O., 1994: *Norsk skoleutvikling etter 1945*. Oslo, Didaktika.

Thrane,V.Coucheron, 1953: De unge menns utdannelse, *Norsk pedagogisk tidsskrift*, s.53.

Vallet, L.-A. and Caillet, 1996: Les eleves etrangers dans l'ecole et le college francais. Une 'etude d'ensemble. *Les Dossiers s'Education et Formations* 67. Paris: INSEE.

Vangsnes,S.1967: "Rekruttering av artianere og karakterer til examen artium", *NAVF, Utredninger om forskning og høyere utdanning*.Melding nr.1, Oslo.

Weeks, A., 1986: *Comprehensive Schools, Past, Present and Future*. London, Methuen